FLAME IN
MOTION

Also by Denise Stewart is:

Finding the Way; A Journey Through Abuse, Therapeutic
   Brilliance and Blunders to Healing (2005), Gazelle Press,
   Mobile, AL 36619

FLAME IN
MOTION

DENISE STEWART

WestBow
PRESS
A DIVISION OF THOMAS NELSON

WestBow Press books may be ordered through booksellers or by contacting:

WestBow Press
A Division of Thomas Nelson
1663 Liberty Drive
Bloomington, IN 47403
www.westbowpress.com
1 (866) 928-1240

Because of the dynamic nature of the Internet, any web addresses or
links contained in this book may have changed since publication and
may no longer be valid. The views expressed in this work are solely those
of the author and do not necessarily reflect the views of the publisher,
and the publisher hereby disclaims any responsibility for them.

Certain stock imagery © Thinkstock.
Any people depicted in stock imagery provided by Thinkstock are
models, and such images are being used for illustrative purposes only.

Unless otherwise identified, Scripture quotations are from the King James
Version of the Bible. Scripture marked LAB are taken from the Life Application
Bible, New International Version, Tyndale House Publishing, Inc., Wheaton,
IL and Zondervan Publishing House, Grand Rapids, MI C 1991. Scripture
marked NRSV is from the New Revised Standard Version Bible and ASV from
the American Standard Revised, Thomas Nelson, Inc., Nashville, TN 37214.

ISBN: 978-1-4908-1346-2 (sc)
ISBN: 978-1-4908-1345-5 (hc)
ISBN: 978-1-4908-1347-9 (e)

Library of Congress Control Number: 2013918672

Printed in the United States of America.

WestBow Press rev. date: 11/04/2013

CONTENTS

ACKNOWLEDGEMENTS

Therefore, as it is written, let him who boasts, boast of the Lord.
—I Corinthian 1:31 LAB

And just as we have born the likeness of the earthly man,
so shall we bear the likeness of the man from Heaven.
—I Corinthians 15:49 LAB

I thank God for who He is in my life and for sending His Son to die so that my sins are forgiven. I thank Him that I am eternally reconciled in intimate relationship of prayer, praise, worship and deeper revelation of my Heavenly Father's perfect love, plans, purposes and will for my life. I thank God for the gift of His Holy Spirit to help me grow each day that I may become more like Jesus, the resurrected Christ, my Savior and my Friend. I am more aware everyday that my righteousness in and of itself is like filthy rags without the saving grace of Jesus and His righteousness in me. My works are futile without faith and the power of the Holy Spirit preparing the way and guiding me. My love is surely lacking without God's love first being poured into and through me. I am also more aware everyday of who I am in Christ, that His blood covers me, and that my Heavenly Father sees me filtered through the perfection of His beautiful, spotless Son, the Lamb of God, Jesus! Hallelujah! God's immeasurable love for me, and for all of us, is manifested ultimately and everlastingly through the finished work of Jesus on the cross. In His love, I pray, 'Lord, help me surrender to you that I may become more like you. Open my heart and my spirit that you may shine your light through me and through these writings, in Jesus name and to your glory. I give you all the praise for you are the King of kings and Lord of my life! Amen.'

I also thank God for all of those in my Christian family who seek His truths and seek to be more like Him. I thank God for His not easily broken, three-stranded cord in my marriage, for my loving and supportive husband, Jerry, for the wonder of our beautiful daughters, Julie and Heather, for the joy of our awesome grandchildren, Skylar and Nathan, for my precious Grandma Coffman who led me in the ways of God and was a wonderful example of letting her light shine for Jesus, and for my family in all the houses of faith that God has blessed me with wherever He has led me. I thank God for influential women and men of faith who have touched my life profoundly with His love and truth. I thank Him for those from my NY church, Full Gospel Tabernacle, including: Bishop Tommy and Pastor Wanda Reid, Pastor Aimee Reid–Sych, and Pastor JoAnn Angelo. Through their love, wisdom and guidance, I have truly experienced a church family who live out their vision of "One people, one call to heal the broken" as they embrace an atmosphere of worship and usher in the presence and anointing of the one true living God who breaks yokes and sets the captive free. These servant leaders also encourage the unique plans God has in every life to live out His Kingdom purpose within us. I am also thankful for Charter Oak UMC, Doctor David and Judy Eversdyke and their influence on my faith walk since I was a young teenager. I am thankful for all of those who took a shared vision with Pastor

Dave and ran with it to firmly establish one of the largest United Methodist bodies of believers in Southwestern PA whose heart it is to actively love God, love each other and love the world. I thank God for my new church family, Word of Life Ministries, and for the love and acceptance in this nondenominational body of Christ. It is a blessing to receive Pastor Tom Walters and Pastor Sheldon Moore's uncompromised focus on the Word of God as well as their open hearts to the Holy Spirit and to freely pressing into self-abandoned worship of our Heavenly Father. These ministers of God's love and church bodies represent what being a flame in motion is all about—sharing God's love and plan of salvation to bring people into healing grace and kingdom purpose to further spread His truth and love to others around the world! (God is so awesome!)

I pray, 'Lord, bless each one according to your riches in Glory. Show us your perfect love and plans for our lives, help us to obey and to live in the unity of being one with you, and fill us with your peace as we live in the victory of Jesus, the resurrected Christ. Thank you for our salvation through the shed blood of your Son who knew no sin. Forgive us when we fall short of your glory and thank you that your grace is sufficient. Your grace and our open hearts are all we need to be intimate with You. Help us, Heavenly Father, to enter into your presence and find peace and rest like secure little babies all snuggled up in Your tender, protective, all-knowing, and all-loving arms and help us also to shine like stars in the universe that you may be glorified in your Kingdom that is and is to come. Hallelujah! In Jesus precious name, I pray. Amen.'

INTRODUCTION

Humble yourselves, therefore, under the mighty hand of
God, that He may exalt you at the proper time, casting
all your anxiety upon Him because He cares for you.
—I Peter 5:6–7 NRSV

As I write, I have been going through a long season in my life of being crushed and stepped on like grapes intended to make a fine wine. My marriage had, for an intense season a few years ago, been through the winepress. This time of preparation has been for all that God has for us in our three-stranded cord that is not easily broken (Ecclesiastes 4:12). There have been huge amounts of internal and external changes and transformation. Thankfully, love that never fails covers a multitude of sins. Even as far as we all have come, we are all works in progress. The good news is that God is the author and finisher of our faith and He will be faithful to complete the good work He began. Personally, I feel somewhat like the Apostle Paul on His journey to love others, encourage Christians, support the church and various ministries, and stand for Jesus declaring the good news of salvation and doing this while writing papers, letters, books and whatever God has for me to write regarding Him or some truth that I feel in my spirit that I need to share. Like Paul, there are times that I feel so much pain when my actions and words are misperceived and I dig in deeper with God crying out for Him to help me, heal me, have mercy on me and let it be His words that I share with you so that I may count it all joy to the glory of God. I pray to God that once He is done pressing me into what He wants that I will be like fine wine filled with the Holy Spirit and ready to be who God has for me to be within His plans and purposes for my life. Similar to the wedding feast where Jesus turned water into wine, I hear God tell me that He saves the best wine for last! Praise God! I declare and decree His best wine for my life and for your life as well! Amen!

In receiving the wine, none of us is perfect. No author or pastor on earth has arrived to perfection. Not one of us even has to be perfect. Look at Paul and where he came from. He went after Christians to destroy them and their profession of Jesus as Lord and Savior. Paul was not one of the original chosen disciples of Jesus, yet he suddenly saw God's light and was transformed. Following his transformation and inspired by the Holy Spirit, Paul was chosen to write the majority of the New Testament regarding the Good News of Jesus Christ. His influence over the establishment of churches throughout numerous regions was extensive. I could list and tally up some estimation of the land Paul covered and the documented churches that he planted. I could also note how he followed up with their ministries along with the way he encouraged believers to grow closer to God through the good news of the resurrected Christ, but I will leave those places up to your own Biblical exploration as we look at being present day flames in motion.

Considering my own life, there are estimated eighty–some churches of predominantly Protestant and also a few Catholic denominations that I have participated in or served as a part of in some way even while, in all of our moves, I have only been a member of five churches in my lifetime. I am not a pastor of a church, although I have recently received my ministry license. I am also not a worship leader, although when God's anointing comes upon me as I surrender more fully to His glory, there is a song in me that I believe God makes pleasing unto His ears. While this Presence of God shines forth, I am most thankful that God keeps His promise to inhabit all of our praises. I appreciate the encouragement from others and, together in unity; we are boasting only and all the more of our Heavenly Father. Even in this act of worship, we are His flame in motion.

While not currently a church pastor or worship leader, I grew up desperately seeking God's love, wanting to know more about Him, and hoping to share these things with others. Not influential as Paul, but like Paul; God has moved me through so many areas and so many churches to share whatever He placed in me to give and to receive. The amazing thing is that none of us know the extent of how we have been used or how others have touched us in the ways that are purposed in God's perfect plans. I just go where God leads me and in my smallness and fumbling around to connect with the people I meet, I do as I sense God wants of me. So, in approximately eighty churches I have touched lives and been touched by others who do not always remember me or me them, yet who often do remember and will always live out that one small way then and again that God touched us through one another. The estimated count of churches does not include anywhere else I have been and all the places any of us with a heart for God go throughout our lives. There are many amazing memories where I need to savor God's greatness. At the same time, my heart aches and my spirit grieves many relationships and shortcomings—my own and others. Yet I believe that we, the carriers of God's glory who have been set apart to bear His likeness, have made the difference that God sent us out to make.

We do so as we participate in the path He set forth before we were even conceived in our mothers' wombs.

In the still moment of pondering God's purpose for my life, my first book, *Finding The Way*, with over 2,000 copies having found their way around the United States and a humble two or three hundred books internationally and now my second book, *Flame In Motion,* in the process of being published; I wonder what God will inspire me to write that He has yet to make experiential in my life and what He will do with this writing. As declared in 1 Peter 5:6–7 at the beginning of this introduction, what I am doing in this process is to humble myself under the mighty hand of God that He may exalt me at the proper time while I cast all my anxiety upon Him because He cares for me.

As we begin and as I type this introduction, I Peter 5:6–7 describes the season that I am in. Have you ever been where there are those who have come against you, where you feel set apart, misperceived, used to make someone else feel bigger or better in whatever way they need and even feeling cast out in some ways? Best of all though, I have experienced old things passing away and new things, situations, relationships and love embracing me like never before and through it all I praise God even in times of grief and uncertainty because He is worthy! The Apostle Paul had a journey and it was not all pretty, but His joy was in the Lord and the joy of the Lord was His strength. We all have a journey of which we are accountable to God. Let us humble ourselves and cast our anxiety upon our Heavenly Father that He may care for us and exalt each of us at the proper time by His mighty hand.

Whether you are in the thick of an amazing mountaintop experience or in a desert of testing, let us take these next moments to rest in God, humble ourselves under His mighty hand, cast any anxiety upon Him and trust Him to fulfill His promise to exalt us His way and in His timing through praying in Jesus name.

Talk with Him even now for He is waiting to talk with you. He is waiting to shine His glory through you. Ask God to open your heart to Him. Be as real and transparent as you can be with your Heavenly Father. He knows the secret places of your heart anyway and loves you just the same. Unveil yourself before Him and let Him shine through you because YOU (_____) ARE HIS FLAME IN MOTION! *And the God of all grace, who called you to His eternal glory in Christ, after you have suffered a little while, will Himself restore you and make you strong, firm and steadfast.* (I so need that promise from you now, Lord!). *To God be the power forever and ever. Amen.* (I Peter 5:10–11, LAB)

—*Denise Stewart,* 2012

CHAPTER 1

Unveil Your Beauty:
Set God's Flame in Motion

Therefore, I urge you brothers, in view of God's mercy, to offer
your bodies as living sacrifices, holy and pleasing to God—this
is your spiritual act of worship. Do not conform any longer to
the pattern of this world, but be transformed by the renewing
of your mind. Then you will be able to test and approve what
God's will is—His good, pleasing and perfect will.
—Romans 12:1–2 LAB

And we, who with unveiled faces all reflect the Lord's glory,
are being transformed into His likeness with ever-increasing
glory, which comes from The Lord, who is the Spirit.
-II Corinthians 3:18 LAB

When I think of Adam and Eve hiding after the throes of their original sin (Genesis 3), I think of the ways we hide and, more specifically, the ways I hide. On October 17, 2011, as I traveled to a Christian event featuring speaker, singer, and comedian Kelita

1

Haverland, I sent a text to my mother in the Lord. She is not my biological mom or even my spiritual mom, though she used to care about many aspects of my life, and we used to share things spiritually. She is the person I considered to be my mom for a season in 2011 and 2012, and I had hoped forever. I felt she and I fit together heart-to-heart as mother and daughter, like I could fully be myself and belong as God made me in my relationship with Mom. We were two peas in a pod. I shared my perception of my childhood and where I learned to hide so well as a result of various experiences with her.

I sent her a text once that said, "Everyone helped themselves to everything in my house growing up—the food off my plate, my toothbrush, my bike, my toys, my jewelry, my underclothes, my money, my privacy, my body. And so I had to hide stuff. Because of sexual abuse by my biological father, I had to compartmentalize and hide part of my heart, thoughts, and experiences that have made a huge impact on my life. Sometimes I have been deeply withdrawn from the shock and the shame-filled parts of my life, parts that I felt too ashamed to share or that it seemed others did not understand no matter how much I tried to tell them. Organizing helps me focus and remember things, especially when I am tired or not used to wherever I am. I organize my head—thoughts and writing—and my things related to packing and unpacking. (I often stay overnight at my daughters' homes. I stayed at my mom-in-the-Lord's house, in my dorm at the Bible school I attended, and I often vacationed. I especially love the ocean.) Managing the drugstore taught me to organize shelves according to planograms and end displays of seasonal items and sales. Jerry (my husband) is organized and likes things clean. Me? I just plain love you, 'Mom,' and I am thankful you make room for me the way you do, however I am. Xoxo."

My mom-in-the-Lord's love and acceptance demonstrated how God loves us, except God and His love are perfect beyond any human limitation. He sees our hearts, and He loves us with an everlasting love. Nothing can ever separate us from God's love once we choose Jesus as our Lord and Savior. Our heavenly Father will never leave us or forsake us. God knows everything about us, like Jesus with the Samaritan woman at the well described in John 4. Jesus told the woman everything she ever did and offered her living water (eternal life). All that she had to do was believe in Him as the Messiah. Jesus knew everything she ever did that fell short of the glory of God, and yet He loved her so deeply that she ran off, telling everyone about Him. I, too, know a man who told me everything about myself, and He loves me just the same. He loves me, and He loves you so much. All we have to do is receive Him.

So yes, Jesus loves us—this we know. But do we? How often do we hide or think we are hiding? In due season, God brings everything to the light. He tells us who we are, asks us who we think He is, tells us everything we ever did, and offers us living water. Jesus offers us His love, His life, and eternal life through Him. He sees us in our nakedness and shame. He heals the broken places, inviting us to go and sin no more and to shine His light wherever God sends us. You see, I know a man who told me everything I ever did and who loves me just the same. Do you know such a man? He is the Messiah, Jesus! I am reminded of His love even now as I feel His presence with me and want to bow down, cover my face, and cry out to Him. But He, in all His glory, lifts my chin in His hand, looks deep into my eyes, sees my heart, and says, "Yes, My love is for you too." How about you? He is saying, "Yes, I love you!" Whatever other gods are out there, this is the God I serve. This is the Father who delights in me and sings over me, even though in and of myself, I know that I am not worthy. This is the almighty God who hides me in His shelter and gives me His perfect strength when others come against me, discount me, misperceive me, and reject me. This is the Savior who calls me higher—not to hide me from who I am but to hide me in His love, to take me to the secret place where it is Him and me, and to fill my cup to overflowing with living water when I feel most dry and thirsty. Jesus is the way, the truth, and the life. I call to Him, and He hears and sees me. He comes to make a way where there seems to be no way and to put rivers in the desert. Praise Jesus!

I just want to stay in the secret place with Him, and so I will for a minute. I choose not to let the world crowd in or obligations to complete this book rob me from this place. Be still and know that He is God. It is okay to take a quiet moment with Him. We need the quiet just as much as we need to cry out to Him with our hearts. We need to soak Him in just as we need to sing out praises to Him. Everything is okay. Though the world comes crashing in on us sometimes, it is okay to be still with Him. It is good for us to rest in God's shelter. Give Him all of your cares and anxieties. In due time, He will lift you up on eagle's wings where you will run and not be weary.

Precious child of God, take a breath, be still, and rest. It is okay to stop and cast your cares upon the Lord. Jesus, during His time on this earth, did so. He went aside from the crowds and spent time alone with our Father. He also spent time with the closest of His friends to pray together with God in their midst. Why do we so often fight this quiet time with Jesus? Are we hurting more than we think He is able to love and care for us? Are we too angry and disappointed in God to stop being ever-vigilant to the things going on around us? Do we think the world cannot revolve without us? Are we afraid of letting go of something to walk with God? Are we afraid that we may have to lay something or someone at the foot of the cross and let even that thing, habit, or person that we love go? To pour out, you need to receive; to receive, you need to pour yourself out. Maybe here and now, while no one is looking, we can take a deep breath, let go of everything, just surrender it all. Maybe we can receive Him and let God touch and heal all of the places in our hearts that need His healing power and cleansing blood to flow, touch, and purify.

Holy Spirit, come and touch us with all that You are and with all that we need. I pray in Jesus's name. Amen.

Be still and know that He is God. Listen to His heartbeat. Listen for His heart-to-heart conversation with you, often known as "His still, small voice." Some will say, "I don't hear anything." It is okay. Sometime you will. There is nothing to be afraid of. It is not time to run but to be still. Whisper His name, "Jesus, Jesus, Jesus—" Jesus loves you. Be still and know that He is God.

This place we have just experienced—separately yet in unity—is an example of healthy hiding. When it is time to come out from that moment of intimacy with Jesus, you may want to shout words of praise and thanksgiving to the Lord. Go ahead! Christ died so that you could be free! Even if you cannot hear Him, God loves you. His love for you is expressed throughout the Bible. Try to picture Jesus nailed to suffer and die on a cross in humiliation and pain. Jesus sacrificed His life out of His love for you and His heart's desire for a relationship with you. Laugh and cry tears of joy. Give sacrificial praise with any tears of pain—surrendering the walls of false protection while reaching out to Jesus! Sing a new song! Our God is so great! Praise Him!

We praise you, Lord! We exalt You! We glorify Your name! God, You are so awesome! God, we worship Your majesty! We laugh with joy, and we cry, surrendering to hope in You and in Your love for us.

Go ahead and be open with God. Don't let me stop you, but

5

I do need to tell you something. I have needed encouragement because of some personal things going on in my life, and just about the time I was going to start writing about us praising the Lord, my husband brought the mail. To my surprise my local Christian TV station, Cornerstone Television, sent me something unexpected. Jerry opened the little box and handed me a prayer shawl made in Israel. I had no idea this special gift and a bottle of anointing oil harvested from Perry Stone's olive grove in Israel were coming to me. I want to talk about Israel later, but at this moment, I have placed the prayer shawl on myself and anointed my head and hands for this writing so that it would bless you and shine a light for Jesus around this world. In all of our praise and thanksgiving of God's goodness, please pray with me for the peace of Jerusalem,

> Lord, we come before you, in unity, to obey your Word and pray for the peace of Jerusalem. Lord, God, they are Your chosen people who seek You for the coming Messiah. Yahweh, Jesus has come. He is the light of the world. He will come again. We will see our Risen Savior in the Holy Land. He is our Prince of Peace, our Shalom, nothing missing, nothing broken. We are whole in Him. Almighty God, I pray for the peace of Jerusalem. Let no weapons formed against Your holy city prosper. May all of Israel remain fully independent, sheltered and leaning wholeheartedly upon your triumphant return. Come, Lord Jesus, come. In Jesus' name we pray. Amen.

God is so good! Why would we ever deny Him or hide from Him instead of resting and hiding in Him? How God longs for us to snuggle up with Him. Rest your head on His chest and listen to Abba/Daddy's heartbeat. Isaiah 49:13–16 LAB says,

> Shout for joy, O heavens; rejoice O earth; burst into song O mountains! For the Lord comforts His people and will have compassion on His afflicted ones. But Zion said, "The Lord has forsaken me. The Lord has forgotten me." Can a mother forget the baby at her breast and have no compassion on the child she has borne? Though she may forget, I will not forget you. See I have engraved you on the palms of my hands. Your walls are forever before me.

Take a deep breath and let it go. God has us.

There are seasons when I have felt set apart and separated from God and others important to me in my life because of some trials He is bringing me through; however, God's Word is good, and He promises me that "though my father and mother forsake me, the Lord will receive me" (Psalm 27:10 LAB). God even has given me instructions. While I may want to jump in and *fix* things right away so that the suffering that goes along with the situation will be diminished, God tells me to do the following: "Wait for the Lord, be strong, take heart and wait for the Lord" (Psalm 27:14). We cannot always count on people because people are fickle, but we can always count on God. People can say they will love us forever, and the first time we express something to them that is hurtful to us, they can cast us out in a blink of an eye. God reminds me, "Wait for the Lord, be strong, take heart and wait for the Lord." God sees, hears, and knows that when we are doing something for Him, that is exactly the time when the enemy wants to use those we love to take us down. This means that we must be doing something right.

Thank you, Lord!

God is faithful. He just gave me a prayer shawl and anointing oil from Israel! Even in the midst of suffering, I can experience joy and praise God! What a way to wait for the Lord! Be strong, take heart, and wait for the Lord by remembering His blessings and praising Him through all else. Honor God in all you do, praise Him, and watch Him work. Taste and see that He is good! Oh, what an *awesome* God who holds us in the palm of His hand and comforts us through it all!

While I am still genuinely smiling from ear to ear with joy in my heart regarding God's goodness, I want to offer an example of unhealthy hiding in our world today. In contrast to what I am experiencing right now, a child may have to put on a smile all of the time no matter what happens to her. People may sexually abuse and take advantage of the child with the pretend smile through parental inversion (setting the child's self aside to take care of parents' needs). Shame, fear, deep wounds, pride, and not knowing a way of escape may keep the child suppressed and oppressed while the boy or girl hides the truth of how badly he or she is hurting. The girl, for instance, may decide that she is rough and tough and that she is made of steel so that nothing anyone does can hurt her. No one knows just how much it takes for the child to function and to accomplish the goals that she has set for herself. Trying to find her way out of the situations by seeking the truth may have only served to leave her deeper in the pit of her difficulties and despair. The longer it takes to find more favorable circumstances for healing, the harder it is to trust that there will be such a support system, and even God seems like an extension of those who have hurt her. The more exhausting the search for healing becomes, the deeper the void grows. Her defenses only serve to falsely protect her from further pain when no one gets her suffering or her as a person. The child feels alienated when all she wants to do is belong and run forward, completely healed, delivered, and set free to fulfill the plans that God has for her. Therefore, she walks around with a fake smile stretched across her face and a quick wit to make everyone laugh so that no one knows and can further hurt her more than she thinks she could possibly hurt and still live. She does what it takes to succeed, even though her appearance of overcoming comes at a cost. Knowing what is going on inside of herself and in her life, the child may feel especially ashamed around Christians—most especially when she hears all about God and how she is supposed to feel His joy and shine His light. She knows only what she sees—the smiles others bring on Sunday mornings and how that compares to her life—only serving to increase her shame and sense of isolation. So the child compares her insides to others' outsides and pushes down the pain all the more. She expresses what she is told God wants from her and wonders how many others are putting on smiles rather than finding the joy that comes with being real. People compliment and genuinely encourage her, but she wonders how long she can keep up the front until the secrets erupt and *they* (or someone who she hopes to trust) learn all of the ugly truths about her and the things that have happened to her. The child grows up trying to be good enough and sometimes acts as if she is too good or better than others just so that she can like herself. She longs for intimacy, but she is afraid of that which she longs for and often feels lonely. The family rewards her successes and the accomplishments that make them feel proud, but they feed on her need for their love by insisting that she pleases them no matter what is going on inside of her. If she steps out of the box that she has been put in, they find a way to criticize her in the places where she hurts and lash out at her weaknesses (even if these are not really weaknesses but the individual and unique way God made her), and they quickly put her back in her box of serving their needs. Who is she? That is what she wants to know as she desperately does what she can to take swings at the statuelike mold that others have shaped her into, a mold that encloses and suffocates the life out of her. She runs away from others in fear of them finding out the truth about her, and she does her best to excel in the gifts God has given her. In those ways she finds freedom. There are those who sometimes look at her like she is different or as though she is rejecting their love, while others actually see her need and pour love and encouraging compliments upon her. She savors everyone's love more than they know. As she grows older, someone tells her about boundaries, and she renegotiates such boundaries in relationships. But she is quite lacking in grace and polite know-how. The child loves deeply and desperately does not want to lose anyone she loves. When she tries to speak up about these things, no one knows what she is trying to talk about as they convey a message to her in one form or another that she is too deep or expecting too much. The child grows weary, but God is faithful. His strength is made perfect in her weakness. Again and again, He is her saving grace.

Feelings are not the enemy. We all have them because God has feelings and we are made in His image. Our emotions are messengers that help us find judgments we have made against others, leading to the root of our pain, the choices we make, and how we relate to others. Expressing our feelings in prayer allows us to have the intimacy that opens our hearts for God to love and heal us along with allowing others to love, accept and validate us. Talking with God frees us to overcome rather than act out our feelings on others. We do not need to be led by our feelings, but we need to see them as indicators of what is going on in our hearts. It is better to seek God's forgiveness for the painful attitudes we have inside of us and to seek His truths through the Bible rather than act upon the attitudes and the emotions that slip out, whether we think we are in control or not. The results could be even more painful to face up to if we burden our children with them and pass the sins and wounds down through the generations. The truth sets us free. Jesus sets us free. See, *I met a man who told me everything about myself, and He loves me anyway. Jesus!*

Let us pray: Heavenly Father, bring Your light to our lives and shine it on everything You want to heal just like You did for the Samaritan woman at the well. Lord, bring healing to our hearts and pour Your love and joy inside of us to overflowing, for Your joy is our strength. Let nothing hinder us from the plans You have for us because we are the hope of glory. We are the vessels that are to shine Your light to dispel the darkness. We are Your flames in motion. Thank you, Lord. In Jesus' name I pray. Amen.

Be careful what you pray because God does hear our prayers and is pleased to bring the shortcomings and hurts in us to the forefront for refinement and healing, and others are certainly willing to take part in us facing and feeling our pain because they do not want to deal with our stuff anymore. Others are more than willing to throw Jonah off of the boat for not going to Ninevah in the first place. Most people will not suffer our pain and how it reflects itself in our relationships for long. They, too, will throw us off the ship and into the mouth of the great big whale, which spits us onto the scary shore where we are supposed to be in the first place. Sure, there are those loved ones who will walk alongside of us because they are family or lifelong friends, but there is the one and only God, our Creator, who will not forsake us and who is without human limitations. God is faithful to complete the good work He began in us, even if it means He is right there out in the middle of nowhere in the belly of the whale with us. God knows exactly where we are going to land when we are thrown out, spit out, and scratching our heads, wondering about what He wants of us, what we did wrong, how we could possibly comply, and if we really have to obey as we make our way to shore?

Like Jonah, we sometimes try to just blend in with the crowd going their way. We try to hide. We try to numb ourselves by sleeping, or sleepwalking through life. We may not be able to cry when the tears are so bottled up and shoved down too deep, causing emotional anguish that begs for an outlet. We have all kinds of feelings. We may have mixed feelings that are like mixed fruit—some we like, but the fruit we do not like is taking away from the fruit we do like. Who wants pain, confusion, uncertainty, fear, or anger? Take this cup (this pain) away, God. I pray in my own way and have cried out to God at times through the years. Take it all away and leave me with the fruits I love and enjoy. Let me only think on those things that are lovely.

Cutting free from others who are not good for us or who are not in God's plans for us is painful. The fruits of the Holy Spirit do not include just joy. There can be long-suffering that produces Godlike characters in us. I love people. I want all of my relationships—well, maybe not all anymore because I am growing tired of being a martyr. Some relationships leave me with such a mix of joy and turmoil as I remember the fun and laughter and also the games of manipulation and pain. Sometimes, like those on the ship who had to face Jonah's consequences for disobedience, I am not interested in always being at the other end of consequences for others' bad choices, and so I choose to throw Jonah overboard for God to deal with. I can only walk my relationships out as lovingly as possible, and so I cry out like Jesus did in the garden of Gethsemane, 'take this cup' even though our cup does not compare to His cup or the rejection, humiliation, beatings, suffering, crucifixion, death and all the things we did to Him. Still, God wants us to come to Him in our suffering and share with Him those things that stir up emotion in us. God wants all that is within us emptied out before Him so that He can fill us back up with all of Him. Like with Jesus on the cross, God makes good out of what men intend for evil, and His glory shines through us. Refueled and refreshed by spending time in His Word, meditating in prayer and praise with our heavenly Father, and sharing with others who care about us, we can remember how much we love everyone and can enjoy the good things from others, whether we can be in close daily relationship or be satisfied loving some people from a distance.

We are only in control of ourselves, and so Lord, I for one surrender my mind, will, and emotions to be in alignment with yours, my heavenly Father. In Jesus' name I pray. Amen.

In 2011, I was in a class at Bible school, one that questioned if we had parts of our hearts that were disconnected from God and others in unhealthy hiding that rob us from love. The course encourages a new freedom and joy in living. The book we used was titled *Hiding from Love* by Dr. John Townsend (co-author with Dr. Henry Cloud of another great book titled *Boundaries* that was also part of our studies at the school). In reference to the sexually abused child in my example toward the beginning of this chapter, how can we let our lights shine if we have been boxed into corners, if we are unable to risk letting love in because of injuries from previous relationships with significant people in our lives, and if we do not have an ability to set true and necessary boundaries and establish healthy ways for guarding our hearts? I remember how difficult it was in sharing my first book, *Finding the Way: A Journey through Abuse, Therapeutic Brilliance and Blunders, to Healing*, published by Gazelle Press in November of 2005. In it, I wrote,

> My struggle with overcoming childhood
> sexual abuse has been both difficult to contain

and difficult to share. The sensitivity of this moment, my brother's death, leaves me yet with other questions about sharing such personal information—information that touches more lives than simply my own. This information touches the lives of family (biological) whom I love and feel deeply bonded to. It is difficult to weigh what is best as I desire to provide some unspoken words and allow God to use me as a vessel in providing His healing touch in other people's lives. I hear voices of those who have similar shared experiences crying out to me to speak the words and finish the sentences. In this writing, I surrender trying to be in control of such a task of weighing the potential fruit, and perhaps the pain, of my words. Instead, I ask God to help me tell my story in a way that touches lives and moves all of us to a closer relationship with Him and to deeper and greater levels of healing. ... While protecting the genuineness of my journey for a greater cause, I have also had to risk exposing myself in ways that are generally private and extremely self-protective. (Stewart 2005)

Chapter 11 in *Finding the Way*, "Moses Speaks," reveals yet another level of vulnerability related to exposure and letting God's light shine through me as a testimony to who He is and God's hand and power in my life as I seek, with all of my heart, to follow Him. Moses first tells God that he cannot go to Egypt on behalf of those held in captivity because he is not an eloquent speaker. Moses does speak, though, and His message is similar to mine when he makes a stand for God on behalf of the Israelites, who had been enslaved and oppressed in the land of Egypt (see Exodus 3–6). Moses declares, "Let my people go!" Here and now I ask, "Go where?" Go to where we are free to be who God made us to be through living out the kingdom plans and purposes He has for us. Press on toward the goal that leads us toward heaven (see Philippians 3:13–14). Read God's Word and allow Him through Jesus to take root and transform our minds and our lives (see Romans 12:1–2). "Go where?" Go to where we are free in Jesus. Go to where we can share in His love with others. Go to where God's light shines. Go and let His light shine through me/us. Just as Moses declared to the one who held them captive, I declare to the captor of our world today, "Let my people go!"

What is your story? What is your test that provides you with your testimony? What needs to be unveiled in you? What are you hiding in an unhealthy way as we pray for the veils to be removed from the eyes of unbelievers so that we all may know the truth that sets us free? Knowing the truth that Jesus gave His life for us so that we may be reconciled and set free, I pray now:

God unveil my beauty, take off the ugly things, and sanctify me through the Holy Spirit. Grow me. Make me more of who you formed me to be when you formed me in my mother's womb and knew the plans you had for my life from even before my conception, in Jesus name. Amen

You see, from out of God's womb, we share His blood, and we become the infectious and by the Holy Spirit of the living God, the contagious carriers of God's love. In God's goodness He does not just leave us where we are at. Instead God works with us and purifies us for His purpose and His glory. God puts us through the winepress sometimes. He puts us through the fire where the dross is burned off and the gold is purified. God disciplines us as His own children because in accepting Jesus as our Lord and Savior, we become God's children, and He loves us. Love matters most, and even when the process is hard, God loves us. Yes, Jesus loves us and gave His life for us because God so loved the world. Whatever is going on around us and whatever anyone else is doing or how the enemy uses others to try to stop the good work that God is faithful to complete in us, no fleshly motive born of sinful man can compare or stop whatever God wants to do. His will already exists and will be done in Jesus' name and to God's glory.

Read the Bible, ask our Creator to make His eternal truths come alive in you, and then seek what God's will is for your life—His good and perfect will. How did Paul write so many books of the Bible and establish so many churches as He shared the Good News of Jesus Christ with the people along his travels? He did so one day and one step at a time. God's blinding light shone upon Paul and transformed him. Then Paul set forth hearing God, obeying Him, and doing what God had for him to do each day, day after day, and that is the discipline of faith that we walk in if we love God and seek to trust and obey Him.

Does what Moses did in the Old Testament, what Paul did in the New Testament, and what we do each day line up with the mind of Christ as written in His Word? Do we keep God in the center of everything we do? I once participated in a Beth Moore study called "Jesus the One and Only." Has Jesus become your one and only? The teacher asked this question in class and here is my answer: "Jesus is my one and only because so often it is and can only be me and Him. There is no other who loves me so much they could take one of my sins let alone all of them as Jesus did when He laid His perfect and beautiful life down to be crucified for me. He loves me in all my imperfections and in places that no one else can reach inside of me. Jesus is my one and only, my best friend, my Lord, my Savior and all that I need Him to be in my joys and my sorrows. I never want to be without Him, and I give Him all the glory for being my way, my truth, and my life. When a mother is not faithful, He is. When a brother is close, He is closer. When I feel the loss of another, He fills me up. My heart burns for Him ... literally. I love Jesus. I laugh with Him. I cry with Him. I fall at His feet. I fall into His arms and pour out my heart. Thank you, Jesus! I was born the only daughter of seven children, and my biological mother would call me her 'one and only.' This affectionate title helps me embrace all the more intimately the concept of Jesus being our "one and only." In His love for us, Jesus went to the cross where He allowed His very blood to be shed for us. Through His DNA, we are each unique yet made in His image, the one and only child of God. He sacrificed Himself and laid down His life for you and me, individually and all together His one and only."

From this place where we find our identities in Christ through His Word, how do we move forward in letting His light shine through us? What it all comes down to in allowing God to unveil our beauty and set His flame within us in motion is as simple, challenging, and heartfelt as a song I (and many of us) learned as children in Sunday school. If you know it, sing along.

This Little Light of Mine

Verse 1
This little light of mine, I'm gonna let it shine.
This little light of mine, I'm gonna let it shine.
This little light of mine, I'm gonna let it shine.
Let it shine, let it shine, let it shine.

Verse 2
Hide it under a bushel, No! I'm gonna let it shine.
Hide it under a bushel, No! I'm gonna let it shine.
Hide it under a bushel, No! I'm gonna let it shine.
Let it shine, let it shine, let it shine.

Verse 3
Won't let Satan blow it out, I'm gonna let it shine.
Won't let Satan blow it out, I'm gonna let it shine.
Won't let Satan blow it out, I'm gonna let it shine.
Let it shine, let it shine, let it shine.

Verse 4
Let it shine 'til Jesus comes, I'm gonna let it shine.
Let it shine 'til Jesus comes, I'm gonna let it shine.
Let it shine 'til Jesus comes, I'm gonna let it shine.
Let it shine, let it shine, let it shine.

Harry Dixon Loes, Public Domain.

CHAPTER 2

Commit Your Work to the Lord

"For I know the plans I have for you," declares the Lord, "plans to prosper you and not to harm you, plans to give you hope and a future. Then you will call upon me and come and pray to me, and I will listen to you. You will seek me and find me when you seek me with all of your heart. I will be found by you, declares the Lord, and will bring you back from captivity."
—Jeremiah 29:11–14a LAB

Therefore, my dear brothers (and sisters), stand firm. Let nothing move you. Always give yourselves fully to the work of the Lord, because you know that your labor in the Lord is not in vain.
—1 Corinthians 15:58 LAB

In declaring that Jesus is the Lord, I know the declaration is greater than me. He is the Lord of everyone and everything. Every knee will bow and proclaim Jesus as Lord, but even our proclamation does not make Him the Lord. He simply is. The implication of this in my life is that He is in me and I am in Him. I am supposed to be who I am in Jesus wherever I go. I am to be a contagious carrier of His love, His truths, and His ways. I want to know Him more and move more fully into the life's plans and purposes He has for me by coming closer to Him as the Holy Spirit draws me nearer. I embody Him. I seek to hear His voice and trust, obey and act upon what I hear in alignment with the Bible.

One of the most amazing things is that with Jesus as the Lord of my life, I get to be the hope of glory that shares Him with the world around me. I get to be His flame in motion as I once wrote about in a poem. The indescribably best part for me, though, is the intimacy I share with Jesus—the love relationship I have in which I can share anything in my heart and He loves me with an everlasting love. He takes the thoughts that I have in my mind so that He can renew and transform me into His truths. He forgives me when I get off track and shows me His will as He promises to shine a light each step of the way. Jesus wants me to live life abundantly and walk in His higher ways. He wants this for me and for the good of all those He loves. My favorite part is the forgiveness of Jesus that connects me with my heavenly Father, who is a "Father to the fatherless" (Psalm 68:5 LAB). I can rest in His arms and find everything I need from my perfect Father, who never leaves me or forgets about me. "Jesus is Lord" means that Jesus is at the center of all things in my life, and I am awed that He wants to be at the heart of me. That puts me right where He wants me to be—totally dependent on Him—now and through an eternity of everlasting life with Him.

What helps me keep Jesus at the heart of it all? I try to obey what Jesus wants of me and to commit what I do to God so that my works succeed. While I was writing my first book, *Finding the Way*, no matter what I went through or had to work out in my own salvation and life experiences, I tried to keep Jesus in the center and commit my works to God so that they would succeed. I wanted to give myself to God in this way as an act of love and worship to Him. It is important to me that what I have to share is within the integrity of who I am in Christ. I seek to be as humble and full of mercy and grace as God would have me be without losing God's way for me and an authenticity of situations and circumstances. Reading God's holy Bible helps me to know Him and how He wants me to live. Sharing God and the things of God with others helps me come alive in Christ. I have fallen short, but by His grace I am saved. Every day there are reminders to keep my eyes on Jesus. I see Him in what my friends and I have written on Facebook, the pictures of Jesus and other items that I have placed throughout my home, the open Bible on my desk and other books I read to learn more about Him, the TV channels and music stations that share about Jesus, the CDs, the DVDs, the conversations about Him with others, the praise and worship music I listen to, the songs God puts in my heart to sing, praying alone or with others, being a part of ministry classes, reaching out to help someone as Jesus would have me do, praying for others, being still with Jesus and others, sowing money into His kingdom, leading where God would have me lead, following God through others where He would have me follow and simply giving someone in need a cup of water in Jesus' name. *Even more than doing, it is about being.* Through the years I have done a variety of things to serve Jesus, ranging from helping clean a church with my grandma to forming and leading a women's Bible study to being a campus minister for a semester. No matter how much I give or how fruitful I am, God blesses me with even more of Him in the fulfillment and joy of who He is in me—Jesus, the heart of it all.

In Psalm 37:4–6 LAB it is written, "Delight yourself in the Lord and He will give you the desires of your heart. Commit your way to the Lord; trust Him and He will do this: He will make your righteousness shine like the dawn, the justice like your cause to the noonday sun."

Psalm 37:5 has been written that if we commit our works to The Lord, they shall succeed. In the King James Bible this verse is written in the following way: "Commit thy way unto the Lord; trust also in Him; and He shall bring it to pass." This same verse is written in the Living Bible (Tyndale House Publishers, 1971) as follows: "Commit everything you do to the Lord. Trust Him to help you do it and He will." I smile at this promise while I think of so many times that He has helped me, and I found myself tearful even just yesterday as I prayed and heard Him in His still, small voice tell me that He would help me. I surely need God's help, and I am not afraid to admit it or to give Him all the glory.

In the book of 1 Kings, Solomon committed his life's work in obedience to the Lord, and his commitment led him to success. Solomon had a strong start, but later chose deliberate disobedience and fell short of the glory of God. It is so important to keep our hearts right with God, but it is also difficult when life gets in the way. In 1 Kings 8, Solomon dedicates the temple, and I think of how much I love the glory of God. I love being in His presence; especially corporately with others! First, God dwelt in the tabernacle Solomon built. (The Tabernacle is also the name of my New York church, where I loved worshiping several times a week and just being in God's presence with my family there.) Then the ark (of God's presence) was brought into Solomon's temple as a symbol of the throne, and the actual presence of God in His house was beyond comprehension. God watched over His house and kept His covenant with David. The priests praised God. The Lord inhabits the praises of His people. "But thou art holy, O thou that inhabitest the praises of Israel" (Psalm 22:3 ASV). The presence of God's glory was the distinguishing mark of the nation of Israel, yet we all sin and fall short of the glory; however, by grace, we are saved thanks to God's New Testament covenant through Jesus Christ's death and resurrection. By 1 Kings 11, Solomon had taken on foreign wives that led him to worship other gods. Even though God had warned King Solomon twice, Solomon "held fast to them in love" (1 Kings 11:2 LAB). This tells me that not all love is meant to be acted upon and not all people in our lives are to be held fast to in love.

In the fullness of time, God's glory came to earth in the form of Jesus. After our Savior's sacrificial crucifixion, resurrection, and ascension came the day of Pentecost when the glory made itself shown in and through all of us. We, God's children, were baptized in the Holy Spirit as one can read in Acts 2. In the Old Testament, setting up a temple and preserving the glory of God in the temple was such a huge commitment. This act was such a precious and deep spiritual and practical need to invest in and carry forth. Today, we are the vessels and carriers of God's glory, but today we carry His glory and His ark of the covenant in our hearts. I so want to obey God and value His presence inside of me, His temple. We are God's tabernacle and the hope of glory to a lost and dying world.

I remember the first time I was slain in God's Holy Spirit. I was talking to God and saying that I did not want "this" unless it was from Him. If it was from Him, I wanted more. I asked God why His presence was so powerful in me and why He was blessing me with such an awesome gift. He said He did so because I always try to obey Him. As I walk with God, I continue to try to obey Him and commit my works to the Lord, trusting that He will help me succeed just as Solomon did in building the tabernacle. Solomon followed every detail of the outer courts, the inner courts, and the Holy of Holies. (See details in the book of Kings.)

King David prepared the way for Solomon and provided his son with what he needed to build the temple. Solomon began strong in obedience. He committed his works to the Lord, and they succeeded while God was faithful in keeping His covenant. Solomon dedicated the temple to God, so God filled His house with His very presence. And to think that God wanted a house of prayer, fellowship, testimony, and responsibility where there would be obedience is so powerful— God dwells in us. God dwells in me. Thank God for the reconciliation where He sees me through the shed blood of Jesus. Otherwise, my righteousness is like filthy rags. As I think of God removing His presence from Solomon's temple, I think that I could not live a day, not even a single moment without God's presence in my life. As I walk with God, I want more of Him. I love the intimacy with Abba, and I want to obey Him in all that He has for me. Sometimes I grow weary and need to rest in Him, but I always want my life to give God glory. Sometimes the preparation God has been bringing me through for several years now is rigorous, including the way He had been growing me and the challenges I had faced while at Bible school and the obstacles I faced while I worked on my master's degree before that.

God began with removing me from everything I knew and had built around me. He took me to another land. My husband and I lost so much of what we had worked for. God led my children to different faraway places—one immediately and one soon after her graduation from high school. Then what happened? God has blessed us, given us double to triple for our trouble, and He has done amazing things for and through us because that is who God is. He helped us through a time when my husband was sick and his job was beyond the stress that he ever knew before, and then some very important people in my life died. In two years' time, ten people in my family and several friends died. God set me on a course of being a spiritual parent, and the most difficult purifying process happened in my marriage. I had moved from my support system in New York and lost my support system in my new community because of the battle going on in my marriage, and I was often teetering on anemia with two solid months of "women's issues." Just choose one of those things: I lost ten family members to death in two years, most of those in six months, and it goes right over people's heads the impact that had on me and on my family as I watched those I loved also in pain. Choose another: Living in a hotel out of suitcases and loaded down cars for four and a half months, driving back and forth to New York, selling our house ourselves, moving in and out of the hotels every weekend. Choose another one: Imagine me, a five-foot-three woman holding up a husband who is over six foot while rushing him to the hospital or following the ambulance as he described how he could not breathe and started losing his ability to stand or walk. There are other scenarios to choose from. I watch people cry over some things and think that they do not have a clue; however, as I have done all of my life, I care about their pain, and so I am there for them in the best way I can.

I have reached out and loved ever since I was a child and my mother would cry. I would try to be strong so that I could be there for her, but now I am stepping back from everyone's expectations and laying down the burdens so that God can restore me because it is His strength that will lift me back up and help me thrive as I continue seeking to obey Him and give God His glory. I have had many costs, but it does not take King Solomon's tragic story of turning to disobedience to encourage me to remain faithful to the Lord. It is God's faithfulness to me that encourages me to remain faithful to Him, and the truth is that I just plain need Him. I need to be at peace with resting in Him. I am desperate for Him! And I believe that the Lord always accomplishes His purposes!

DENISE STEWART

The thing I admire most about King Solomon's life is that he was committed, dedicated, and determined to serve the Lord and to do everything to the specifications that God wanted. What stands out to me about his disobedience is not what he did wrong as much as I understand what it feels like to just get tired of doing everything so meticulously right. For example, I am a good, organized, dedicated, committed, responsible student, but I sometimes wanted to throw up my hands and say, "I don't want to write another paper or take another test or show up for class or sleep away from my home or gracefully deal with anyone else's drama or sit still through anyone else's power trips or whatever it is. I could be with God somewhere on the beach and that would be a good plan—a great plan." However, I don't think that would have been God's best plan for my life, and I want His best plan. I want Him to say, "Well done, good and faithful servant." So the only way I can follow this path for my life is to press into my love relationship with Him, fall at His feet, shout with praise other times, and put one foot in front of the other as He shines His light at each step of the way because I am following that light, His light within me, whether I have to walk, run, or even crawl. And sometimes He has to just plain carry me. Praise God! When God is carrying me, that's when I have committed everything to Him and He is helping me accomplish His plans for my life. He does promise to prosper us and give us hope and a future.

I did not know what I was doing when I wrote my first book, *Finding the Way*. The writing had to come out of me because keeping it inside was overwhelming me. I kept putting the writing away, and God kept urging me to bring it back out. He had me comparing my heart and thoughts to stories and verses in the Bible and aligning my painful and self-destructive thoughts with His truths. God took me to a church that encouraged me in who I am in Him and in the destiny that He has for my life.

He told me I had a lot to learn on a spiritual level and He would be with me. I am not an English major, and I was afraid of computers, so writing a book is a complete other process God brought me through. Then the question became this: How do I get my writing published?

I began searching through books and the Internet to learn about publishing companies. I would listen to those in my church who published books and see what they did. I chose a few Christian publishing companies online and saw what they required for manuscript submission. My focus continued to stay on committing my work to the Lord. I told Him again and again that I did not know what I was doing and that I needed Him to show me, open doors, and do it. I did what was in my power to do at any given moment. I felt small in my relationship to others who succeeded in ministry, writing, music, or whatever they brought when it came to the gifting God gave them and shared at my church. I did not give up or back down, even though so many times I wanted to. I did not have a family background that opened doors for me or showed me how to succeed. It was God, Jerry, and me moving forward as God showed me what to do.

Imagine—I was an incestuously abused kid from a little town, and I was now in this big church in another state, surrounded by men and women of God. At my church I also came in contact with visitors who were well-known, televised ministers and evangelists. I stood in praise and worship before the pulpit of Bishop Tommy Reid, who is a well-connected man of God, once on the boards of Oral Roberts University and Pastor Cho's ministry, who has been on several Christian TV stations, hosts *Living Epistles,* and has regularly been on *Ask the Pastor.* And there I was! What did I have to offer? I had what was in my power to do. I had this writing that I wanted to publish. Pastor Tommy, as many lovingly call him, a man who has been a spiritual father to me and many others, would stop and talk to me as if I was somebody. I told him I felt so small, and he told me that God brought me there to show me that I am not so small. I told him I had a book I wanted published, and he gave me a few gems of information. I watched, praised, prayed, and worshipped until everything eventually unfolded and I had a book in my hand with my name on the cover. God opened the doors and paved the way. It is all His doing! Glory to God!

"God," I asked, "what do I do with this book?" I am not comfortable standing in front of people and speaking. I compare myself to Moses talking to God about not being an eloquent speaker. *But God* showed me how to sell some books, get a tax number, set up displays, and retain the courage to talk with people even while my book included sexual abuse. So I had to overcome the sense of shame in that taboo area of life in order to have conversations with people. I shared my book with the Women's Bible Study. I literally sang the "Little Drummer Boy" to the women, then described my book as giving my best to Jesus just as the little drummer boy played his best for Jesus, "pa rum pa pa pum." You see, if I give what is in my power, even if it is a small thing, then I have to have faith that God will do the rest. I played my song for the newborn babe in the manger and believed He would do miracles, teach, establish His kingdom on earth, and reconcile us into eternity with the heavenly Father, who loves us with an everlasting love. I had my little book as I watched other ministries flourish while I said, "God, I don't know what to do now, so You'll have to promote this book." It was about then that God opened the door for us to move back to Pennsylvania, and so I was stepping away, though not apart in love and spirit, from my New York family. God gave us a beautiful home, and I asked God what I was supposed to do with the remaining 2,500 books I had sitting in my house. I looked back at a professor who laughed at me and said my book was *Vanity Fair.* He said that he had boxes of books sitting in his basement, and I said, "No way."

One day, I was praying, and God gave me a vision. I saw myself standing on the mountain where I lived in Central Pennsylvania. The elevation of the mountain is high in contrast to the surrounding areas. As a point of reference, Johnstown (where the historical flood was located) is at a much lower elevation and is south of where I stood on this mountain. I was turning in all directions, passing out books like a speaker on a stage would toss them to the congregation or whoever his/her audience is. I was tossing books down the mountain on all sides, and so I asked God, "How will I do this?" I needed others hands to help me. I would give my books to people at that point—to friends, conference speakers, whoever I felt God led me to—but one day, God showed me how much we traveled and how there were Goodwill stores everywhere. God revealed to me how it was a new fad to shop there and these stores served as a refuge for people suffering hard economic times over the past couple of years. Where else could they get the kind of deals they wanted and needed there? I discovered—surely at God's prompting—that there were hundreds of Goodwill stores everywhere we went, and we rarely ever had to go off our route to find them. My husband, Jerry, and I traveled throughout numerous states in the United States and in some parts of Canada, and on our way to various places, we would drop ten, twenty, or thirty books off and trust God to distribute them to the people He wanted to have them. Once on the way to our vacation for our thirty-second wedding anniversary, we dropped off two hundred books at approximately seven Goodwill locations. During our drive my hand felt really hot, and the heat lingered. I touched my neck and felt something move. I felt a little silly, but also that I was to touch my husband's back and pray for healing. Jerry had been having back pain and was going regularly to a chiropractor for adjustments and whatever was needed to relieve the pain. We had been to a Holy Spirit Seminar weeks before where he was in pain struggling to stand up in the pew for healing prayer. At that time, I placed my hand on Jerry's back and there was no change. This time when I placed the heat from my left hand on Jerry's back, God healed him that very moment on August 18, 2010! My husband went from being in too much pain to help unload a shopping cart and lift his luggage into the car to being fully healed! So do not despise small beginnings in the ministry God gives you because God has many ways of blessing us in our obedience. Two and a half years later, Jerry has never seen a chiropractor again. Not long ago, during some cold temperatures, we and our younger daughter carried many loads of drywall, DRIcore flooring, insulation, and floorboards into our basement, which my husband and I planned to finish together. Recently he framed and we hung drywall on the walls and ceiling of our basement. I do not know exactly who was touched during our unique distribution of *Finding the Way* as God led us. I do know that Jerry was touched by God's Holy Spirit through my hand that day. Glory to God!

In the meantime while my name was not a well-known one, God led me to give books to so many whose names are recognized in ministry. This kind of marketing has not traditionally been the world's way of doing things, but it was the way God showed me. Rather than feel embarrassed that my way was unique, I realized that my topic was difficult and taboo and perhaps there were people who needed to be reached behind the scenes where I know I am most comfortable. So any glory that comes as a result of anything linked to my writing belongs totally to God. I boast of the Lord, Jesus Christ, of the Holy Spirit, and of the God of the universe, my heavenly Father, and of what He does with that little thing that He gave me to do.

Dear Father God, help us be obedient to your will and your ways no matter how unique the path is that you take us on. In Jesus' name I pray. Amen.

Through the lesson of King Solomon (described earlier in this chapter) and how he started out obediently following after God as his father, King David, showed him, we can see that he lost his way. Solomon, in all his wisdom, chose disobedience through marrying women who did not worship God. He had been fruitful in building the temple only for it all to become meaningless. What is the difference between King David and his son, King Solomon? King David sinned but turned back and repented in obedience to God. Still, the Lord always accomplishes His purposes. No matter the sins of man and the waywardness of Solomon in building a temple for the Ark of the Covenant, the Son of God came down through the throne and lineage of King David, the imperfect man after God's own heart. He was born to save the world just as God had planned, purposed, and promised. There is no one like our God! Commit your works, your ways, and everything you do to God, and He will help you. "Therefore, my dear brothers (and sisters), stand firm. Let nothing move you. Always give yourselves fully to the work of the Lord, because you know that your labor in the Lord is not in vain" (1 Corinthian 15:58 LAB). Amen.

From this place where we find our salvation, identity, and purpose in Christ and where we commit our works to the Lord, how do we move forward in letting His light shine through us? In Dr. Bill Hamon's book, *Apostles, Prophets, and the Coming Moves of God*, I learned some things about the process and preparation between calling and commissioning. Matthew 28:19 talks about the "Great Commission," where we are to go into the world and make disciples. We are *all* called to make disciples through the power of the Holy Spirit, given to us in the early New Testament church and also in these days as described in Acts 2. For me, my way of reaching out right this moment is by staying up and tapping the keyboard with the words God gives me. We all are given something in our hands to do. Some are called to pastor a church, but we all have this commission in one way or another. In chapter 6 of Dr. Hamon's book, he gives us examples of David, Elisha, Joseph, Abraham, Paul, the disciples, and Jesus Himself all having been called and the process and preparation that occurred over the years in each of their lives.

Briefly, the first thing that happens regarding a ministry we are called to is just that—God calls us. Second, we respond yes or no. If we say no, God works in us to say yes, but He will eventually find someone else to replace us in His plans and purposes if we do not move forward with Him. Third, God qualifies the called to build the necessary foundation for quality, quantity, and lasting ability of the ultimate ministry. In this process, the greater the preparative process and deeper the preparation, the greater the person and ministry can be. The process is in place by God "to root out and to pull down, to destroy and to throw down, to build and to plant" (Jeremiah 1:10). David maintained an appreciative and humble attitude through the twenty-four-year process of being called to serve as king to actually being a king. He remained faithful and true to God. Fourth, the phrase "it is darkest before the dawn" is applicable to a person about to come into his/her ultimate calling and destiny. And five, don't give up! David encouraged himself in the Lord, so you should maintain integrity and faith. Wait for God's timing. Do not settle for partial fulfillment of God's prophetic destiny. Endure and receive prophetic promises. Know that a divinely called one cannot bypass God's process. The trying of one's faith is more precious than gold. Sixthly, press on in fulfilling your ultimate destiny, fully committed to keeping God in the center of all you do. Even as I edit this book, I know my life is definitely not a piece of cake. A whole lot of things came up that have been so painful, but while they did not take me out, I had to rest in the Lord until it was time for Him to lift me up. Whatever the process is, God can faithfully bring us through. Commit your work to the Lord and never give up! Remember our little Sunday school song? "This little light of mine, I'm gonna let it shine. Let it shine, let it shine, let it shine." It's all about Jesus! Let Him shine through you!

CHAPTER 3

Remain in My Love

Jesus said to His disciples, "Before long, the world will not see me anymore, but you will see me. I am in my Father, and you are in me, and I am in you. Whoever has my commands and obeys them, he is the one who loves me. He who loves me will be loved by my Father, and I too will love him and show myself to him."
—John 14:19–21 LAB

I woke up one morning with emotional pain in my heart, the same pain I went to sleep with the night before. Have you ever noticed how people flock to other people who have been marked by life because of something they have done or because of the type of family they have been born into? Such people can say that their puppies had accidents on the carpet, and so many people want to be right there in the know and in the 'higher places.' I am sorry to confess, but even I want that too. I want to belong and to be loved. I want the love that overflows from my heart to be received purely in the way it is freely given. Is not that the heart of God as well? Is it not the cry of His very own heart to belong, to have His love received, to be purely received and freely given? Is my cry so different from His? "Choose me! Choose me! My heart aches for you! Please, choose me!" So I stop a minute from aching because my love does not always make it into the "in" person or group. Sometimes my heart of love is ignored, twisted, perverted, mistaken, rejected, and even slandered. Does this sound like David in the book of Psalms? Even the very people who are supposed to reveal God's love to me occasionally break my heart. So I stop. I stop trying. I stop to rest. I stop to see only *Him*. I stop to remember once again that God *is*. God is the Creator of *all*. He was here before Genesis. He created all created things ... ever. He is the God over ministers, ministries, presidents, governments, educators, educational systems, patriarchs, matriarchs, families, worship leaders, worship songs, worship ... *all*. When I feel left out or when I just need to get away, I pause for God, and He meets me where I find comfort ... in the quiet rest of His love.

Be still with Him and make this be your heart's hunger and call to God as well. Worship the Creator and say to yourself, "He also created me, chooses me, and loves me with an everlasting love. He is jealous for my love, comes calling on me for my love, my love that others would trample, not unlike the crucified Savior of the world. Come and save me, Abba, Father! Come and save me, You who are jealous for my love. Father, even the idea of loving You can only exist because You first loved me. Rescue me from the workers and their good works so that I may feel your genuine, perfect, and pure love. Show yourself to me. Hold me in Your arms. I never want to remain anywhere else. Praise You, Lord, God Almighty, Maker of heaven and earth, Abba, Father, Jesus, Holy Spirit. Do whatever it takes to keep me in Your steadfast love. There is nowhere else in all of your creation that I would rather be than soaking You into the very depths of my body, spirit, and soul, soaking in, soaking in, soaking You into me, Lord. I choose to remain in Your love. You are faithful.

My help comes from You, Lord. *Never* let me go, in Jesus' name. Amen."

This is what Jesus says,

> I am the vine; you are the branches. If a man remains in Me and I in him, he will bear much fruit; apart from Me you can do nothing ... This is to my Father's glory that you bear much fruit ... I have told you this so that my joy may be in you and your joy may be complete. My command is this: Love each other as I have loved you. (John 15:5–12 LAB)

Lord, make your joy complete in me as I remain in You!

Lord, it is one thing to love You with all my heart, mind, body, and spirit and another to love others as You have loved me. Look what was done to You when you came to love and give life more abundantly. Look at what we have done to You ... at what I have done to You. I am humbly abiding in You, seeking to be Your flame in motion, the hope of glory as a vessel of Your love. You have hovered over the mountaintop where I lived, and I realize that You hover over all the mountaintops, watching, loving, waiting for that moment I look down and away from You—not because I do not want You or because I do not long to remain in You but because I am humbled by Your presence. When you return again, it will surely be just as Your Word says, "At the name of Jesus every knee should bow, in heaven and on earth and under the earth, and every tongue confess that Jesus Christ is Lord, to the glory of God the Father" (Philippians 2:10–11 LAB).

I write these things to You, Lord, that You will be fruitful in me. You are the vine, and I am a branch who longs to love You, love others, and bear fruit. Apart from You, I can do nothing. I want Your fruit to last! I want Your joy in me so that my joy may be complete! Your joy is my strength! I need You! What am I looking for? Where can I go from Your love? Who am I apart from You? Apart from You, Lord, I can do nothing. In You, remaining in Your love, I can do all things through Christ, who strengthens me. Glory to You, heavenly Father, and may all the earth sing Your praises. Go before me, Holy Spirit. God, I love You. Help me to share Your love. Unveil my beauty and set Your flame in motion. To Your glory, Lord! Amen.

During ministry after class on September 16, 2010, I was called forward for prayer and reminded that God is a gentle Father, and then another minister was called forward to pray for me. She told me that what happened to me as a child was wicked. She prayed for me that the fortress would be removed from my mind and that I would be refreshed. She then laid her hand on my stomach and spoke *release*. That prayer ministry opened up a layer of pain in me that I knew would be exposed prior to even coming back to school that fall, a pain that God wanted to heal. I felt such a mix of excitement and nervous energy that I could not sleep some nights the week before school started up again and the first week of my classes. I loved school, and it felt like Christmas to get to take all of the classes. I also knew God was going to be doing something in me, and I was both eager for what He was going to do and nervous with the thought that there would be pain in the process.

At that time God gave me a vision of a sparrow with a wounded wing. As far as I had already come, I still felt I had a wounded wing from childhood pain that held me back. My mom in the Lord had so much love that she poured out, and she gave me a book that night about God's love for me. She was so on target in her timing because I felt so bad about myself that I could not even read one page of the book; however, I could read her message of love, and I was glad that our paths had crossed under God. The next week, in contrast to the vision of the sparrow with the wounded wing, I saw a dove. It was flying around my car when I was on my way to school! It was so beautiful, so pure, so white, and so symbolic of the Holy Spirit living in me. Praise God for His Holy Spirit in the form of a dove.

We can look for personal ways God is speaking to us as we remain in Him. I believe His message for me is to focus on the dove, the Holy Spirit, rather than the sparrow because God sees and He heals broken wings. While my eyes are on the dove, God's eye is on the sparrow. He is taking care of the broken wing. If I keep my eyes on God, He will heal those places inside me that need the touch of His Holy Spirit. As we abide in Jesus' love, we discover that He speaks to us in so many ways, including in visions and dreams.

In a reoccurring dream, a thief would steal everything in my purse, and he would only leave my purse behind. I was so shocked by the fact that everything was completely emptied out of my purse that I had no energy left in me to even know how to gather account and phone numbers and call the bank and credit card companies. I told a couple of people what happened, but it took days for me to sort out what to do and get enough energy to make the calls, even though I knew the thief was running up my charges, draining my checking account and so on. As much as I knew I needed to do something, I could not function, and no one I told could help me. Finally, and with great effort, I found the paperwork I needed to make the calls, but I found out that everything had been maxed out. My inability was holding me back from acting, and the feelings were too overwhelming for me to figure it all out. My energy was stolen. Even when I did make the phone calls, I could barely hold the phone up, get my thoughts together, and dial the right numbers. Finally, I made the calls, but still, everything was gone. This is similar to what it felt like to be sexually abused, trying to figure out what and how to deal with it when it was too late. Everything was stolen. Everything was gone. No one could do anything about it. Beyond that, I had to think of what could happen and the safety of my mother and brothers. When everything is stolen and gone, what does life matter anymore? Maybe it is like when a precious loved one dies and you just go through the motions because you have to. There is no way around it. Then you have to find a way to go on. So it is like my book, *Finding the Way*. "Jesus answered, 'I am the way, the truth and the life. No one comes to the Father except through me'" (John 14:6 LAB). I know that whatever love I have and whatever light I have, it is Jesus shining through me as I abide in His love.

During ministry my brother in the Lord said things to me that tied into the dream. He also prophetically said things related to my crying out to God on my way back up the mountains as I had been praying the previous week to move closer to the Bible school. I had literally and tearfully cried out these very words: "Lord, contend with my contenders." The message I received from my brother in ministry after class was that "God would contend with my contenders," and as we walked around the classroom and laughed together, I was told that I needed "to see myself walking with Jesus" and that "God was restoring what the thief had taken." My brother and teacher did not know any of the dreams I was having or the prayers I was praying. Later he hugged me and let me rest on his shoulder as he encouraged me and assured me that God had handpicked and chosen me to be there. Not only was my faith strengthened, but again, God lifted my eyes away from my circumstances and put my focus on what a powerful God He was who cared about the details of my life.

As I left school for home, I asked God why I had to have things opened up in me regarding the childhood sexual abuse because I thought I was doing fine with it. Just then I saw a truck passing by as I sat at the stop sign. In big letters across the side, it said, "Restore Rite."

Okay, God, I get it. You want to restore these things in the right way.

I put these prayers aside and thought about how tired I was during the traffic and long drive when I suddenly felt the pain come over me again. Just then a truck passed by, one that had written on the back of it, "Residual waste." *Hmmm*, I thought, *God, you are talking to me again.* I felt like the pain and process I had been going through was God getting rid of the impurities that were left after the purifying process that had lasted the previous couple of years.

That evening I asked my husband what "residual waste" was just to get some more information on it. He told me that this waste was composed of impurities that could be buried. People had to dispose of the waste in a proper way. He went on to say that someone once dumped such impurities into a pond and that the pollutants destroyed everything in the pond. I understand what my husband was telling me in relationship to the pain I had been feeling and the healing and restoration God was doing in me. The Lord is faithful not to leave us where we are at but to purify us and flow through us. Jesus may have been crucified, but they could not get rid of Him. Neither will He ever let go of we who have received Him into our hearts as the Lord of our lives as He continues to do good work in us. Let us keep our focus on God in all His majesty rather than the broken places that He does heal. Hallelujah!

Now I will add a little more to the story of the sparrow. Two years later in September of 2012, I had some struggles in a few relationships that were very dear to me. There was just no way around the issues, and I could not take carrying things that did not belong to me. The interesting thing is, though, that the people I was having problems with loved cats. I thought about how much they would love and accept me if I was a cat outside their house. The next day while I was at one of my favorite places with my husband, we were walking along the shops and amusement park area of the beach when I saw a cat holding a sparrow in its mouth. I did not have a good feeling about what I saw at all. When I returned home, it was like an explosion had taken place in these relationships. Within a few weeks things became worse for me, and it took everything for me to function, sit outside, and/or take a walk. I had to move at whatever pace I could push myself forward, and I often stopped to rest in God. When you love deep, letting go is no easy process. Loving God as much as I do makes a huge difference, and I trusted in Him to see me through. It seemed that He was not going to let me move forward with my writing until He brought me through this relational situation. The thing is that God loves me more than a hundred sparrows, and it was time to really turn to Him. In some current situations the enemy had a foothold in my life, especially where I was weak and where he could set me back in future ministry endeavors. God, in His faithfulness, was helping me through in a way that would strengthen me. I can give Him prayer and praise and look to the Holy Spirit, and I have done so; however, this time God gave me some other instructions. He revealed some Bible verses to me, verses that led me to the conclusion that I was supposed to take heart, be strong, and wait upon the Lord. A friend confirmed this when she told me she felt God was massaging and strengthening my heart. With all my heart I want God to help me resolve and restore those relationships. In either case I know this much: God is taking what the enemy meant for evil and making it for good, and again, it is all about remaining in His love.

Whatever is going on with us, God can heal us, restore us, bring us back to Him, use us in a powerful way so that even in all of the cutting, pruning, and remaining in Him, we can bear fruit. One thing that I am thankful for as I consider the life of King David is that no matter what he did, King David remained a man after God's own heart. David committed sins and paid grave consequences, including the loss of his baby that was conceived in adultery with Bathsheba, but God still used him. Wiersbe wrote in his book *Be Restored*, "Even the best men and women in the biblical record had their faults and failures just as we do, and yet the Lord, in His great sovereignty, was able to use them to accomplish His purposes." I love God's heart of forgiveness and restoration when David confessed his sins and turned his heart back to God. Wiersbe writes that David "washed himself, changed his apparel, worshipped the Lord, and returned to life with its disappointments and duties. In Scripture, washing oneself and changing clothes symbolizes making a new beginning." He goes on to say that "Because of God's grace and mercy, we can always make a new beginning."

I know this about God making all things new and giving us new beginnings. I am thankful that God is so merciful and full of grace that He does bring restoration into our lives. He gave David and Bathsheba another baby, Solomon, to carry on and even restore the temple. This is important to me in my own life because no matter what my weaknesses or shortcomings are, I am reminded that God can and does use me to fulfill His plans and purposes. God gives us new beginnings. He cleans and purifies us from the things of the world. Furthermore, Wiersbe refers to Genesis and talks about how the Savior would come through the tribe of Judah, how the Messiah's reign would go on forever, and that "He would be born in Jerusalem, the city of David." Because the reign of the Messiah would go on forever, "David would have a house forever, a kingdom forever, and a throne forever, and would glorify God's name forever. All this is fulfilled in Jesus Christ, the son of David. No matter what depths the kings and people descended, the Lord preserved a lamp for David and for Israel." Because of God's covenant with the house of David, "we today are indebted to David for keeping the light shining so that the Savior could come into the world." For me, no matter what I do or what dirt gets thrown on me to try to blow out my candle, I trust God that He will forever shine His light through me and light each step of my path so that the world may see Jesus shining in and through me. Abide in God because He is not a respecter of persons and He has fruit for you to bear.

God is so awesome and so worthy to be praised. He redeemed the people of Israel from Egypt and set the prophetic truths in every detail throughout the Old Testament to tell of the coming Christ of the New Testament. God performed miracles and drove out the nations and gods that stood in the way. Nothing was going to stop the coming of the Messiah that had been set in motion. God made the people of Israel His very own forever and made a way to redeem us so that we could also be God's own people forever. In wanting us and the intimacy of a relationship with us, He made a way for us to be His people and for Himself to be our God forever. Hallelujah!

On a personal level I described in a detailed way how God is guiding and revealing Himself to me. He uses me even in His plans and purposes pertaining to the return of His beloved Son for the bride of Christ. Even in this one little thing of praying, "God, I pray for the peace of Jerusalem," God is using me for His kingdom that was, is, and is to come. God has made me (whoever I am, whatever I look like, whatever has happened to me, and whatever I have done or not done) to be His very own daughter. That's powerful!

There is no other god like you God! There is no other god who loves us back, let alone loves us first. There is no other God who loves intimacy with us and cares about a relationship with us or who would give His own beloved Son for us as you did so that we could be reconciled to you! Praise you, Lord! You are an *awesome God!* That I am even here praising you is a miracle and reveals your love for me and the way you care about my life and the relationship we share. Thank you, Lord. I humbly exalt you, and I am thankful that in all your majesty, you are a good God who wants us, waits for us, and loves us. How humbling is that!

The Bible verse God gave to me as a teenager, aside from John 3: 16, which urged me to believe in Jesus as the way to everlasting life, is Nahum 1: 7. "God is a good stronghold in times of trouble." I have often reached out to others, but ultimately, I know it is God who is my good stronghold. Ultimately, there are moments when it is going to be God alone with me, when everyone else is doing their own things. He is the one who knows us best and has the most patience, grace, and mercy toward us. He understands us without any condemnation. He knows that we shine as pure gold in Him when others cannot really grasp the race we have run. When my grandmother was on her deathbed, she said at one point, "If somebody doesn't help me, I'm going to die." We already knew we were losing her, but I did not want to say anything because God could extend her time here, so I just held her hand and lovingly looked into her eyes. At one point, I started to let go and walk away; however, she kept hold of my hand, and I stayed close by her side. Later, she said, "My help comes from the Lord." I nodded and shook my head in affirmation. What wonderful words of truth to hear from my grandma. It is true. Our help comes from the Lord, and He is faithful.

God will set us up with healing places, and we are invited to trust His set time for us if we so choose. At times, I feel like I am back in time reliving certain experiences, but I know that really is not true. At least I know that is not true in my head and spirit, but my emotions have not always caught up with the present yet. At fourteen years old when I was sexually abused, I did not really know what to do because everything was over my head in terms of understanding. I did not know what to do to take care of myself. Still, I had to believe that this time around God wanted me to take back the ground for Christ that the enemy had stolen from me in the past and that God had already given me the victory if I just walked it out and let God's power demolish the strongholds as I put my trust in Him. If you are like me, we are not so graceful walking through God's healing process because of so many feelings flooding out—feelings we are to share with God and those He puts in our paths to offer encouragement to one another. God wants to heal us not only for His plans and purposes in our lives that we may bear fruit but also simply because He loves us. God loves you! He wants to unveil the secret places of your heart and heal you, His beloved. He wants to work with you to set His flame in motion through you. Commit your work to God and abide in Him and in God's love because you are His hope of glory, moving from glory to glory to glory. *You are his flame in motion!*

Lord, let us then approach the throne of grace with confidence (Hebrews 4:16 LAB). Help us to run this race that you have set before us. Help us to stay open and soften our hearts to receive protection, rest, and comfort in You, even as you open the door for us to reach out to others. Lord, break off any condemnation that the enemy has schemed against us, trying to disqualify us from making a difference in your Kingdom. Help us to keep our focus on You and what Your Holy Spirit can do rather than on the broken places in our lives. Thank You for going before us in the plans You have for us and for Your glory that shines through us. Thank You that You have called us and chosen us for Your purposes. Thank You, Lord, for You have set us apart and anointed us with your Holy Spirit to do the work you have for us. Thank You for that promises that Your Word does not return void and for Your faithfulness. Most of all, thank You that You love us with an everlasting love and that as you go with us to do the work that You have for us, Your light continues to shine through us. Your love abounds and remains in us as we remain in your love. Jesus, Your name is above all names. In Your name we pray. Amen.

CHAPTER 4

Love Never Fails

Love is as strong as death ... It burns like blazing fire, like a mighty flame. Many waters cannot quench love; rivers cannot wash it away.
—Song of Songs 8:6b–7a LAB

Love burns like a blazing fire, like a mighty flame. Love never fails, and that is who we are as flames in motion. We are God's love in motion. Even though waters may come and try to quench our love and God's light in us, know God's promise that "rivers cannot wash it away." Know that God's love is everlasting. God is faithful. Abiding in His love is living, breathing, and resting in love we can count on because His love for us is enduring love. God's love is not human love even as we are reflections of His love to one another. Even as waters rise, no matter what is going on in our lives, they cannot quench His love because God's love never fails. Thank you, Lord.

The following is from a pragmatic sermon I developed for a Bible School online class that relates to God's promise that love never fails. The text is from Luke 2:1–7 and Luke 2:21–35. Please read the Scripture first to get the full impact of the message

47

titled "Human Suffering and Joy to the World." The question is this: Where is this joy and peace when I have had so much loss and pain?

We may get a mindset that God is not for us. He never has been. We have had to struggle and suffer all of our lives. It may seem that God is not for us in our times of loss and pain. We may ask how we can remain in His love when we cannot feel His love. The problem with this kind of thinking is it keeps us isolated from God and stuck in our suffering. We may say that people do not care. They just think of themselves and take whatever they can. Others may be busy with their own lives or even following what God has for them. If we open our hearts to the ways people do care, we will find that they are there for us more than we realize. We may decide that we have to be out for ourselves and take whatever we can in order to get by in life. Sometimes we feel we are all alone, but I urge and encourage you to take a step of faith and talk to God about how you feel and what you need.

We sometimes think that God is not for us, that He is above us, allowing our suffering and not being there for us, but He came to us in the form of a little baby whose name is Jesus (Luke 2:1–7). Did you ever consider the birth of Jesus into a world that He did not have to enter except out of God's love for us? There was no room at the inn. The Savior of the world met us in a stable manger. Joseph and Mary traveled from Nazareth to Bethlehem to fulfill a census mandate when Mary was ready to have the baby. They traveled dry and dusty "roads" by donkey. They were not married yet by the way, and Joseph was not the baby's biological father, so that created all kinds of gossip and stereotypes, especially in that time and culture. When Jesus was only eight days old, they had to travel again by donkey. They went to the temple in Jerusalem because it was mandatory that every firstborn child be circumcised, named, and presented to the temple. Joseph and Mary also had to gather and give a sacrifice while they were at the temple. Joseph, Mary, and Jesus happened upon an elderly man who recognized that the Savior had been born and blessed them and left this thought for the young girl, the new mother of a firstborn child, to ponder: "This child is destined to cause the falling and rising of many in Israel, and to be a sign that will be spoken against, so that the thoughts of many hearts will be revealed and a sword will pierce your own soul, too" (Luke 2:34–5 LAB). Just as Jesus, who was born in a manger, met us where we were at in our hearts, God has met you where you are and has always been there for you.

See John 10:10. Sin has opened the door for destruction. We can stay stuck in the consequences of sin or focus on Jesus, who came that we could have abundant life. In John 11, Martha and Mary thought Jesus had abandoned them, that their friend did not care to come and help their brother, Lazarus. They felt the pain of death, loss, hopelessness, and they felt like God did not care, like the one who could help them did not bother to show up until it was too late. We can think people do not care because they do not meet our expectations, but God's ways are higher than our ways. We can choose to keep our focus on Him no matter what because He is a good God who cares for us. Even Jesus wept because of their pain and suffering. In Exodus 3:7–8 LAB, God says, "I have indeed seen ... I have heard ... I am concerned ... I have come." God does not abandon us. He does not simply leave us to our own means. Do we want to do everything out of human means, turning our backs on God and His ways, or can we turn our eyes and hearts to Him, do what we can do, and believe that He is coming for us just like He came for the Israelites and just like He came to save us from our sins and reconcile us to the Father? Read John 3:16. Do we have to be isolated from God and others? God loves us! God loves you! He sent His only Son just for you!

Jesus came so that we could have life more abundantly through keeping our eyes on Him and intimately embracing His joy and peace within us. Just like us, Jesus came into a world of sin, pain, and suffering. Jesus, as we open our hearts to Him, is found at the center of all our pain and suffering. Jesus came into this world to save us because God loves us. God loves you! Jesus overcame the world, and through Him, we can overcome. Jesus is our joy and our peace in the midst of human suffering. Jesus is the Good Shepherd who is willing to leave His flock and go after the one lost sheep. Is it you that Jesus is reaching out to? If so, I humbly offer a few suggestions for responding to Him:

- Be willing to open you heart to spending time with God.
- Don't hold back. Talk to God and share all of your heart with Him.
- Give praise, even if done sacrificially.
- Listen to praise and worship music.
- Sing along until you get lost in God's joy and peace.
- Read verses in the Bible of God's love for you.
- Do something to show God's love to someone else.

In that same class I also had to write a declarative sermon that was also useful in regards to this truth of God's unfailing love. Consider Peter 3:13–20, "Being Set Apart." The biblical truth is that if you are for God, you may need to let go of some people you love in your life. You will still love them if you have God's love in your heart, and we still need one another; however, there is no one like our God, nothing like living in the plans and purposes He has for our lives and not one who can bless us with the joy and intimacy we share with Jesus when our sins have been forgiven and we have been cleansed with His blood of righteousness. A popular song by Chris Tomlin is titled "Our

God." Part of the lyrics talks about how God shines into the darkness and how awesome and powerful He is. If God is for us, nothing can stand against us. There is no one like our God, but not everyone chooses Him. Some even, intentionally or not, are against us. Some try to pull us back into the darkness. Some stand in the way or try to stop us. So let me ask you this: Are you willing to let go of those you love for the sake of your love relationship with Christ?

There are those who God has us separate from. It is not because God would have anyone to perish; it is a matter of free will and making a decision to follow God. For example, God had a call on Abraham's life that set him apart, but Abraham's nephew, Lot, chose to come with him, even though Lot was not choosing God. Among many other difficulties, Lot was a part of the sinfulness of Sodom. Abraham prayed for God to save Lot when God revealed that He would soon destroy Sodom. You may think that you will be a godly influence and that it would be good to have the familiarity of your family member by your side. You may think that it does not matter what Lot does until one day you realize that if your loved one is not for God, they are not for you and will bring you useless suffering. There are those from whom God has separated us.

There are also those whom Jesus invites that turn their backs on Jesus and walk away from His invitation to receive Him as the Lord and Savior of their lives. It is not that others are deprived of the same opportunity to follow Jesus as you or I do. It is that some choose not to believe, and so they simply walk away. One of the greatest miracles of Jesus occurred when He multiplied the fish and loaves of bread and fed the thousands. He called Himself the "Bread of Life" and required the followers there that day to believe in Him as the true bread from heaven that gives life to the world. The disciples were to eat of this bread of life

(Jesus) to receive eternal life. Many of His disciples chose not to receive Jesus as the Bread of Life. They turned back and no longer followed Him. You may be a believer who stayed while others, many being those you love, could be those in your family, who walk away. There are even those who have been fed by Jesus yet refuse to do what is required and believe. There are those who walk away no matter how much you love and want your loved one to join with you in your belief of Jesus and commitment to remain in Him. You may not want to let go, but there are those who walk away from Jesus' invitation.

More than being set apart, you may be pushed apart. You may think that no one will harm you for your eagerness to do something good or right, but that is not always true. There are those who abuse others because of jealousy or whatever evil they are willing to participate in. They reject and push away those who are in the plans and purposes of God. In Genesis 50, Joseph was given a dream full of purpose, one regarding the call on his life. His brothers were jealous, and so they plotted against Joseph. They left him for dead and eventually sold him off as a slave to those passing by. Joseph's brothers rejected, physically harmed, and made sure that he was taken far away from the family. Perhaps you may not be physically harmed in God's plans and purposes for your life, but many have experienced words and actions of rejection for their faith in Christ. While God sanctifies us and sets us apart from those in the world, including those we love, there are times when you have to let go because you may be pushed apart.

There are those who just plain think what you are doing is crazy, and they stay away. Some people are so closed-hearted that they totally dismiss what you are doing for God, or they may make fun of you from a distance. In Genesis 6–9, there is the story of Noah and the ark. Noah obeyed God and built the ark, even though there was no rain and no apparent need for the ark. Rather than hearing the voice of God, hearing what Noah was saying, and joining in to help build and board the ark, only eight people were saved through the rising water. There are times when God's instructions make no sense, but we have to obey even when others may laugh, judge, and make fun of us. Like with Noah, we sometimes have to let go of those we love because there are those who just plain may think what you are doing is crazy.

Sometimes the greatest suffering you face is the loss of loved ones you have to let go of during your faith walk with God. Sure, you may see them around and even (1) *pray* for them to believe and follow Jesus, but you may also become stressed trying to hold on like Abraham did with Lot. Or you may (2) *let go and move forward* like Joseph did. You may simply (3) *stand with Jesus* and watch loved ones walk away rather than (4) *believe* that He is the Bread of Life, or you may (5) *find shelter where God has placed you* like Noah and the ark while you are suffering because those you left behind are going to die and there is not a thing you can do to change their minds and get them on your boat. But there is one thing Noah, Abraham, Joseph, and even Jesus have in common. These men of God (6) *know that there is no one like our God*. Noah was saved from the flood. Abraham was the Father to many nations. Joseph became second in command and later fed his family in a time of famine. And Jesus overcame sin and death, and He is coming again in victory! Whatever the path of loss or pain in letting go of loved ones, those named in the illustrations all know the abundant blessings of God to "those who love Him and are called according to His purposes" (Romans 8:28b LAB). Some of you may know the tremendous grief of rejection and loss as you made a stand for Christ, but if you do, then you (7) *truly know as well that there is no greater joy than following God and sharing in intimacy with Him!* (8) *Hold on tight with both hands and your whole heart to that joy, intimacy, and the freedom of knowing there is no one like our God!* You see, if our God is for us, then who could be against us?

As I think of that sermon, God's love, and how He is for us, I remember times my mother in the Lord held on to me as I worshipped and prayed during our ministry time. Once I knew it was her who came alongside of me, I gradually began to rest in her arms all the more. At one point I closed my eyes, and I saw an image of the upper half of my biological dad coming toward me as if he and the sexual abuse were overshadowing me. Not only did I feel the safety of Mom's arms around me, but without me saying a word, she immediately heard from God and spoke about those things He had to say to me about the past and about her arms representing His love and how He has been with me all along. Then the image was gone. It was all about the love and compassion of Jesus coming through Mom to me, and I would not trade those moments of love that I have needed for so long for a million dollars! When Mom showed up and loved me in those places where I have felt unloved and unlovable, it is God's love that came through, and while I became scared that others would abandon and reject me like they have before when I have allowed myself to risk reaching out, Mom pressed in all the more. It was as if she just knew when to be there and what to do. I think it was a season of feeling the love of God through a selfless mother.

How hard it is for some of us to reach out sometimes and say, "I need you," and trust that we will not be neglected, abandoned, and/or rejected. How wonderful to be loved, not for what we do or give but for just being there as part of the family of God that shares the bond of His love together.

Together, let us take a moment and be thankful to God for those in our lives who have walked this love and life out with us and for those who have made a difference in our lives because they have been God's arms of love around us. Some of us have to get through and beyond feeling like we are a bother, unwanted, unlovable, and so on. Mom told me that she wanted me to reach out to her when the enemy was telling me these lies but that it takes time. Like Naaman (See 2 Kings 5), who had to dip in the dirty waters of the Jordan River seven times, healing sometimes is a process, but God gives us His best. Instead of being further hurt, taking time means bonding more, learning that we are here to help one another and feel loved in a lasting way that goes deep inside of us. Trust comes when we keep God first as we share in His love with one another.

I take a moment to pray: Our heavenly Father, You turn the wrongs into rights, for You are good and "we know that in all things you work for the good of those who love (you) and are called according to (your) purpose" (Romans 8:28 LAB). Thank You, Lord. Amen!

As I reflected on my Psalms class ministry time and wrote of Mom demonstrating God's love to me, I saw the Communion bread and juice on my desk at home and chose to take it in remembrance of Jesus, whose body was broken for me. I prayed as the Holy Spirit led me to do the work of God. I recalled those moments in class as though I was still sitting in the classroom. The worship music was very beautiful as it ushered in such a sweet presence of the Holy Spirit to and through those who had come early to pray. God's Spirit moved through others who joined together in the corporate anointing as we entered the classroom. The Psalms were brilliant while the Holy Spirit flowed, pulling us closer in intimacy with our heavenly Father through whatever situation, fear, attack of the enemy, and need for the promises that God has for us. He, our Creator and the genius over all mankind, has us in the palm of His hand and firmly in His care and protection. God upholds us with His mighty right hand.

These songs assure us over and over again that God maintains His faithfulness and that He loves us with an everlasting love in whatever we experience at any given time. The Word of God poetically sneaks in and touches us in unexpected ways as we walk out our lives in faith just as we walked out that semester together. Our teacher offered us an opportunity, perhaps a Kairos moment, to be a witness of God's goodness and faithfulness. We shared the words of the corporate body, the willingness of each person to be vulnerable and humble enough to speak what God had given each of us as we witnessed the story of the Psalms unfold in our own lives. I wondered how poetic I should be or how flowery I should write as I reflected upon the Psalms we shared together. It all sounded so sweet, but like any good Psalm, the semester brought with it both sorrows and joys, struggles and triumphs, and sometimes when God seemed furthest away and unattainable, the faithfulness of our loving Father went deeper and pulled us closer in relationship to Him.

As I was writing my class paper, I could feel the call of God to go deeper and share more. That night I was not sure I had it in me to express the darkest or brightest moments in my life during our semester, but I shared in obedience and waited to see what God would say and do. The truth is that sometimes the process just plain does not sound so pretty or feel so good! Sometimes it is as though God is nowhere in sight and the enemy wants to fake victory just when God shows up and knocks him off his feet. In God's divine order, we read Psalm 10 on September 29, 2011. "Why, O Lord, do you stand far off? Why do you hide yourself in times of trouble?" (Psalm 10:1 LAB).

I stayed for prophetic ministry, and I was reminded that God was doing a new thing and that He is always faithful. Old things have passed away. Over and over, my brother in the Lord spoke to me that God was moving me from here to there, and he moved his hands to emphasize what God was saying. God assured me through my brother that "everything is going to be all right." I wrote this later: "Sometimes something in me could scream, and I do not know what it is; however, the words in the fog of my mind say, 'It's too much. It's all too much!'" In Exodus 3:7–8 LAB, God tells Moses, "I have indeed seen the misery of my people in Egypt. I have heard them crying out … and I am concerned about their suffering. So, I have come down to rescue them from the hands of the Egyptians and to bring them up out of that land into a good and spacious land, a land flowing with milk and honey."

God promises in Isaiah 49:15–16 LAB, "Can a mother forget the baby at her breast and have no compassion on the child she has borne? Though she may forget, I will not forget you! See, I have engraved you (each one of us personally), on the palms of my hands. Your walls are ever before me." I was thankful for my mom in the Lord as I thought of my biological family and how real and horribly rejected being sexually abused by a father and emotionally abandoned by a mother felt. I stood in front of the classroom, looking at the Bible verse that suddenly felt like an evil trick. That night, another woman of a motherly age was there during ministry time. The other woman tried to take charge over me, and she was not the teacher. She was someone who liked to take charge, and that did not go over well with me. I looked at that verse, and a thought came in my mind that I was going to lose my mom in the Lord. Then another thought followed the first one, a thought that I had not experienced in many years. It was this: *God doesn't love me.*

I could not sleep all night, and as soon as morning dawned, I sent this text to my mother in the Lord: "Mom, I've been waiting 'til morning to talk to you. I'm thinking about Thursday nights and I am going to follow your lead and leave after class. I have been so open and exposed as God leads in our relationship and don't think it is good for me to be there without your covering. You are my mom, and I don't need any other woman trying to take your place during ministry. I just want to love as God leads me as I walk in His ocean of love without any riptides trying to pull me under. See you soon as I can. I love you."

Mom replied, "You are my daughter, given to me from God." I cried as I read Mom's words, and then she added, "I am waiting for a hug. I will cover you with God's love."

During another time in class we went around the room, reading verses from the Psalms, and I read the promise from God, similar to Isaiah 49:15–16. I read Psalm 27:10 NRSV, "If my father and mother forsake me, the Lord will take me up." While on some level I was aware that God was exposing a deeper, wounded place inside of me for healing and for the good, all I could feel was that my heart was breaking. I felt myself shrivel in my seat, withdrawing like I was not going to come out and talk to anyone again, that I was going so far inside of myself that I would rather die than risk loving anyone again. I felt like I had lost one set of parents, and if I lost another, it would kill me on every level of my soul. I felt even more certain at that moment that God did not love me. There was a place inside of me where I felt no one could love me, and I knew I could not live in that place of darkness. I thought of how loving Mom had been toward me and how consistent her love had been. The feeling I had was not logical, yet I could feel it like feeling my fingers on the keys of my computer creating the words of my heart and mind. Something was transpiring in the spiritual realm and I knew it to be true even if not yet factual.

I heard my brother in the Lord teaching the lesson, and he said, "It's okay where you are. Just be with the Lord where you are, and He will move you to where you need to be." I risked a note to Mom about what was going on with my heart breaking and how it would kill me if I lost another set of parents. She wrote me a letter back, and in it, she asked if I was staying for ministry or coming home with her. Then she signed, "Love, Mom." God has been healing a wound in me through my relationship using Mom as a vessel of His love. If you never had the absence of such motherly love, then you cannot understand. It is true, though, that we can depend upon God even when it means He sends someone to show us His love. My brother came to me after class as though he had heard my thoughts of not being wanted and said something about us getting together when things slowed down. We hugged. It is so meaningful to me every time he looked at me and called me "Sis" or "Sister." I need God's love through our family, through my brother, and through Mom, and so I went home with her that night.

On October 20, 2011, as sometimes happens when God is doing a work in me that I have to face again, I was struggling with my emotions on the drive to class. I kept hearing the enemy saying that God did not love me and I would say, "He is my heavenly Father, and He does love me."

So the enemy whispered, "Your dad sexually abused you, and he didn't love you. And God doesn't love you."

Jerry and I had gone to hear a Christian singer, Kelita Haverland, at a church near Lancaster a few days later, and I was listening to her music about Bella, a girl who had been sold into human sex trafficking in Cambodia but who had been rescued. This girl was now preparing to become a counselor with the hope of changing the world. Kelita did not know of my struggle when she wrote on my CD, "To Denise, God loves you." That was God showing her what to write to me. This kind of thing happened in class when my brother in the Lord had me read the words off the board at the beginning of class the week before.

God's words to me and to all of us are these: "You are precious to me." I wrote to my mom in the Lord, "Sometimes it is hard to feel God's love, and so I have to think of Jesus on the cross and try to believe I have a heavenly Father who loves me." I cried on my way to school and pressed through during the long drive. Mom encouraged me in God's love.

She sent a text, "Demand Satan out of your life now. I love you." She called for just a quick moment. Never in my life have I experienced someone go to bat for me in such a protective, consistent, and loving way. It was a spiritual battle that Mom saw me through as she stood firm with me, encouraged me to sing of God's love, and prayed for me. I believe she and I put a thousand angels to flight on my behalf, and I could feel God's love and Mom's love in that place that so wanted to swallow me up the week before. I shared briefly after class how the lesson on the board and the words God spoke through my brother ministered to me, and they truly did in an amazing way that could only have been God speaking through him.

My brother in the Lord passed around the message that "God keeps His promises." He said one of his kids had made the message, and it dropped in front of him on his desk. The very next morning, I was sitting at my desk in the dorm and noticed something had dropped on my desk in front of me as well. It was a red rose. I had cut the rose from a calendar and placed it on my picture of Jesus hugging a woman, a woman I perceive as me. The rose never fell before, and it landed on my Communion cups facing me. I had set it on the picture to show my love for God, and He placed it on the Communion wafers and juice cups to show me that He loved me. As I reflect, I realize yet again how personal and intimate our heavenly Father is and how He loves us even in those deep, hurting places that He exposes and brings to His light for healing. I do not think I ever felt His love in the depth of that wounded area of my heart before, and when I needed to know of His love most of all, He reinforced it in so many ways.

As I think of all the ways God has brought me through everything and how He had given me a new family to love and to love me, I know there is joy and blessings in obeying God beyond what I ever dreamed or imagined! I never would have received the gifts of my new family in my life if I had not chosen to obey God and walk out this process throughout my life to get to where I am today! How many different directions could I have taken?

I have to believe that there is more joy, blessings, anointing (that breaks yokes), and love to come. Jesus saved the best wine until last. That is what I think of my relationship with my mom in the Lord and with our family. The best is yet to come—that is what I choose to believe. As the Lord said several times through my brother, God is "moving me from here to here." I see my brother's hands showing me and emphasizing the words. I have to trust and obey, as Psalm 1 says, and I must keep making the choice to walk in God's light, even when it sometimes feels dark because God has shown me once again that He will not forget me. The Lord promises that He will take me up, and so He has as He always does. The first thing God assured me is this: "Everything is going to be all right," and so I believe it is. I love you, Lord! The Lord reminds me that I love Him because He first loved me!

In life everything *but God* changes! God does not change. His promises are yes and amen. Within a year from that time, God gave Jerry a new job. I graduated from Bible school with my ministry license. Both of my daughters moved a few hours closer to us. Jerry and I sold our beautiful home in the mountains, and God had a new beautiful home built specifically with us in mind as He returned us to the town He had moved us from in 1998.

I was so looking forward to living closer to my new family in the Lord, but we came face-to-face with some differences that I tried to communicate to the family. Rather than working through these challenges together, I felt a devastating loss when Mom told me they were ending our relationship. The next tremendous hit I felt happened a couple of weeks later when the dean of the school asked me not to continue in the class I had started because He said some things were being stirred up and someone outside of the school had made a threat against me. I could not believe that the dean was letting that threat stand. I asked him about ordination and he said this would blow over by then and to guard my heart. None of these were school issues. They were family issues that had been building behind the scenes and that I had kept separate from school. Still, I was set apart from the people who said they loved me and the people I love. I was isolated for reaching out and speaking out in the context of family and the ones who said they loved me used the school to remove me. I had just invested my heart and nearly three years of my life in relationship with friends and family of God at the school and was abandoned in an instant to deal with the hurt I felt so terribly that the writing of this book suddenly felt too heavy and was delayed significantly and some of what I had previously written needed to be changed to give a more accurate description of my story. Before I could even move forward with the ministry that God has given me through writing, I had to overcome what had happened enough to write from a heart that honored God's light in me rather than the place in my heart that felt so defeated and diminished. I went from being an excited 4.0 student and president of my little graduating class to fighting an exhausting emotionally uphill battle to overcome what had happened enough to complete this book, then to find out that I would not be ordained because the dean said that writing a book is good, but that I did not have a ministry when the time for ordination came. Still, as had been prophesied, "God moved us from here to here" and yes, just as the

Bible says, "Love … burns like a blazing fire, like a mighty flame." Love never fails, and so I stand on that word in relationship to my heavenly Father. As James Robison and Jay Richards write in their book, *Indivisible*, God "loves us and He sustains us at every moment. Our value comes from this unique relationship. 'For you formed my inward parts/you knitted me together in my mother's womb,' says Psalm 139. God is closer to the unborn child than that child is to his mother." Within this truth I move forward still believing that "everything is going to be all right" because even when it does not feel like it, everything already is all right in Jesus! Thank you, Lord.

I believe God would have me share with you something He once spoke to my heart:

> *Now is the time.* I want you. I have you in the palm of My hand. I breathe the very breath of life into you because I want you. I gave My Son because I want to be in relationship with you. If it were only you, I would provide the same sacrifice so that I could have you with Me for all of eternity. Now is the time for you to know that you are Mine. I want you and I love you. Now is the time for you to believe My Word and My love for you is true and to settle it once and for all in your soul. It is time for you to know deep within you that you are Mine. I bought you with a price, the Sacrificial Lamb, spotless and perfect, because that is how special you are to Me. I have never lost at anything because even in the sacrifice of my Son, the glory, My glory, was at its greatest. For while He suffered death on the cross for your sins; He

was not a loser. While He was rejected by men, He was not a reject. While He was betrayed, He was not defeated. While it looked like all was lost, it was not lost. That day, the greatest seed that was ever planted became the everlasting life of many, as many as the stars are in the universe. I know the plans I have for you—plans to give you hope and a future. Your future is everlasting through the blood of the Lamb. Your hope is in Me. Your help comes from the Lord. You are not lost. You are not a loser, defeated, mistreated out of a sense of worthlessness because you are Mine. You are in Me and I am in you, Christ in you and the hope of glory. I glorify Myself through the resurrection represented in you. Do not try to take my glory by calling yourself less than who you are. You are My daughter, My son, My child, My friend, My chosen one. I love you. These are not mere words. These are My heart for you. While you have your identity in Me, I have My identity in you through Christ, the Son of the living God. Now rise up my child and walk in the victory, for My victory is yours, My child, and the vessel of My glory!

God's call upon our lives is to rise up and shine, for the glory of the Lord is upon us! Amen!

"Love is patient, love is kind. It does not envy, it does not boast, it is not proud. It is not rude, it is not self-seeking, it is not easily angered, it keeps no records of wrongs. Love does not delight in evil, but rejoices with the truth. It always protects, always trusts, always hopes, and always perseveres. Love never fails" (1 Corinthians 13:4–8a LAB).

CHAPTER 5

Love in Perspective

"Come follow me," Jesus said, "and I will make you fishers of men." At once, they left their nets and followed Him. Going on from there, He saw two brothers, James son of Zebedee and his brother John. They were in a boat with their father, Zebedee, preparing their nets. Jesus called them and immediately they left the boat and their father, and followed Him.
—Matthew 4:18–22 LAB

When they had finished eating, Jesus said to Simon Peter, "Simon, son of John, do you truly love Me more than these?" He said to Him, "Yes, Lord; You know that I love You." Jesus said, "Feed My lambs."
—John 21:15–17 LAB

Do not conform any longer to the pattern of this world, but be transformed by the renewing of your mind. Then you will be able to test and approve what God's will is—His good, pleasing and perfect will.
—Romans 12:2 LAB

In order to become who God created us to be, we must cut ourselves free from the things that hold us back. We must sometimes leave our families of origin and former positions to step into what God calls for us to do in our lives just as the disciples did in the scriptural examples above. We are first and foremost God's children, and if we love Jesus, we will do as He calls us to do and feed His sheep as He, the Good Shepherd, leads us to do. This surrender or abandonment of the way we would choose to live comes with sacrifice that is not always easy or without counting the cost. Still, there is joy in the fulfillment of being in God's plans for our lives. As we test and approve what God's good, pleasing, and perfect will is through the renewing of our minds, we will not be conformed to the pattern of this world. The world will not understand. Answering God's call in our lives is definitely a faith walk.

To be a vessel of God's light, we do not have to be perfect. We do have to be willing. We do not have to have approval of man. We do have to be obedient to God. Jesus said, "If you love me more than these—" If you love me more than who or what? Fill in the blank in your own lives. What keeps you from answering God's call or from walking it out completely? Considering the specifics of Peter's life, the challenge Jesus posed could have gone as follows: Peter, if you love me more than fishing for a living; feed my lambs. Peter, if you love me more than being with family on the banks of your hometown; feed my lambs. Peter, if you love me more than hanging out with your friends; feed my lambs. Peter, if you love me more than hanging out in your boat; feed my lambs. Peter, if you love me more than telling fish stories with whoever is willing to listen; feed my lambs. Peter, if you love me more than the three times you denied me; feed my lambs. Peter, if you love me more than your worldly lifestyle; feed my lambs. Peter, if you love me enough to come out of the security and comfort of the boat and walk on water; feed my lambs. Whatever it is, if we love Him, we will feed His sheep in the unique ways

Jesus calls upon each of us to do, and that is a powerful challenge to even dare write about. Only if you have lived what I am talking about will you understand. As for me in this season of my life, Jesus might say: Denise, if you love me more than the Bible school and the family in the Lord that I had given and taken away; feed my lambs. My response is that I love Him as I push through every obstacle the enemy has placed in my life to write the words of my love for Jesus in this book.

Going back to 1997, Jerry and I were at a place in our faith where we both wanted to serve God more. (Watch what you ask for.) In 1998 God had us leave our jobs, our community, our church, our home, our town, our dog, and even our firstborn daughter as soon as she graduated from high school. The ministry that I had facilitated and thought I could utilize in the new state was taken from me as well when the internationally known leader began "leading her flock astray" according to the 700 club. Our finances were very limited, and there was not enough to maintain the life we had. We were unable to collect on money others owed us for the work Jerry had done, so we could not live where we had been raising our children. Eventually Jerry went through the one open door God gave us. In fact, none of the positions he applied for worked out because his area of expertise had been too specialized at that time, and the one opportunity we were offered came when a headhunter contacted Jerry. As my husband began his new position, God began bringing us through a training ground at a higher level in the things of God that has continued even now fifteen years later. In this process, God returned us to Pennsylvania and led me to and through the Bible school to further be tested and approved by God. Eventually, not unlike James and John in the Scripture above, it was necessary to even cut free from some areas of my life that I did not want to cut free from. In my heart I never wanted to leave the area where I grew up when Jerry and I married in 1978. My love for family has always been deep, and so this was hard. And yet it was not our first move, and there have been too many times of having to let go of those I love so deeply. God moved us several times throughout our marriage, and so many times, I would settle in and God would have me lay it all down again just as I was getting established and building relationships. God's ways are greater than my ways, and I have at times felt hurt when our calling would have me let go again and again. Those who had always had their family and foundation in place judged me at times when they had no idea what this felt like. They had their mother right there supporting them in the things of God most of their lives. If they moved, it was often only to get established in adulthood, or they relocated within the area of their upbringing. Some people act like they know something when they have no idea.

When we returned to Pennsylvania in 2006, we were in a different place in our lives—a different town, a different type of church, a different level of income, a larger and newer home, better cars, higher education for me and higher positioning in Jerry's career for him, my first published book, and both daughters had become adults living their own lives, walking very different paths. They both ended up in Virginia around the same time that we ended up back in Pennsylvania. Jerry's network of business associates continued to grow nationally through all of the changes in various fields and roles. I had to walk away from the network within my previous career choice as I moved from social services to more ministry-focused interests. Even while I was earning my master's degree, I sought out an internship in campus ministry by calling a local campus and becoming their first campus ministry intern ever. That started a new beginning for that campus, and their staff started seeking interns each semester after that. I went on a job interview at the University of Pittsburgh at Greensburg before I went to Greater Works Outreach Bible School, and when I came out of the building, I saw a student wearing a sweatshirt from Hilbert College in New York, where I had interned. It seemed to me that God was continuing to encourage me and call me forth into some facet of ministry. It was as if to say that I could go fishing or I could feed God's sheep.

I really did not feel in my heart that the academic advisor position was for me at that time. I just had no idea that God was going to provide a way for me to go to Bible school—even though I had wanted to attend the school since God had led me to the Holy Spirit seminar at the Greater Works Outreach in 2000. God's ways are higher than our ways, and it was a mystery to me why God would move me to New York in 1999, slay me in the Spirit the first time in Tennessee that same year, and bring me to the church seminar in 2000 in Pennsylvania. I lost touch with most of my friends, not because I wanted to but because of the changes as God led me to build relationships with others in New York and in the Pentecostal community of believers. Some family and friends died during my time away, and I grieved while I also felt blessed to be in the midst of some amazing ministries in New York at the church where I experienced the leadership of those who had been spiritual parents to me and so many others, Bishop Tommy and Wanda Reid. While at the Tabernacle, God showed me many women and men who came to our church and spoke from Pastor Tommy's pulpit. What a fascinating world of ministry to show me! I had grown up in a small town, had been sexually abused by my biological father, and had lived in shame for so much of my life. Talk about humility and being humbled. I often did not even know what to say to anyone. I would visit Pennsylvania and talk with friends and family there, and then I would return to New York and close myself off, unless I spoke with close friends in smaller settings. I was loving and playful, hugging and smiling, greeting and pressing in with God, expressing growing pains at the altar even; however, I had a lot to learn, and I closed up to some degree in the process of it all.

Leaving Pennsylvania to follow God's call for me was very painful, sorrowful, and difficult, even though I had prayed to serve Him more and did not understand the cost of all that I would have to lay down. God told me that I had a lot to learn, but He would be with me. God has been faithful to His Word.

Before we moved, God had me help a friend who was battling depression. Other friends brought a Holy Spirit–filled *prophetic pastor* whom I had never met before or seen since, and I had no idea what they were talking about. Just a few weeks before I was supposed to join Jerry in New York, this pastor told me that there was a church in Orchard Park with a pastor named Tommy Reid, and he recommended I go to that church. When he prayed, this man started praying about books. There were things he prayed and talked about that caused me to feel like he knew something about my life and God's plans for me. I had no understanding about prophets in the Bible or how God spoke to us in such a way today, and it made me angry that he seemed to know some secret inside information that was personal to me.

We ended up living in the Northtowns near Buffalo when we first moved to New York, and we did not visit the Tabernacle as recommended because it was located a bit south of us. At the first Holy Spirit seminar I went to in 2000 I wanted to experience more of the freedom I felt in the Holy Spirit and remembered what the pastor at my friend's house had told me. Furthermore, it was prophesied at the seminar that God was taking me away from where I was, and I wondered what that meant as I drove the four hours back to New York. We were renting at the time, and the landlord arrived at our house almost as soon as I did. He had a buyer for the house and offered two months of free rent if we would break the lease and move. We had wanted to live in the Southtowns, and I knew I wanted more of what I experienced at the Holy Spirit seminar. That introduction to the pastor before our move to New York is how I ended up at the Tabernacle with all the wonderful church family and experiences I had there. God works in mysterious ways, but it's key to listen to His guidance and walk it out.

A wonderful example of God's plans for us was going on a cruise with approximately two hundred others from our Tabernacle family along with pastors from other churches and some people from their congregations. Pastor Tommy Reid hosted the cruise in 2007 and invited me to share my first published book, *Finding the Way*, while we were gathered together for a service out in the middle of the Atlantic Ocean. The church leaders, particularly Pastor Tommy, had been teaching me of God's plans and purposes for my life and how God's kingdom resides within us. This teaching was encouragement for me in the pursuit to complete my first book and get it published. It was through the Tabernacle that I assisted in a mission trip to Mississippi after Hurricane Katrina, and weeks after my book was published, I watched a few of my friends reading their copies and sharing it with others around them while flying the friendly skies. The transition in my move to New York was difficult and I quickly became an "empty nester" as a part of that process, then grieved the loss of my precious grandma and other family members who died before God returned us to Pennsylvania. Still, I look at all God opened up for me and count my blessings.

God was good to bless me with the joy of grandchildren before He took my grandma home to be with Him. God was faithful not to leave me or forsake me. Instead, He drew me closer to Him. As God draws us nearer to Him, to rest in Him, growing more intimate with Him is every bit as much a part of being a flame in motion as writing a book or giving a sermon or spreading God's love to someone in passing. It is through pressing in with God intimately through prayer, praise, worship, and Bible reading that He fills us with His love, and only in that way can we pour out from what He gives us. Being a flame in motion and receiving His love burning for us is the only way to keep moving forward as we surrender to God's will and His plans and purposes for our lives.

In considering the chapter heading "Love in Perspective" and the Bible verses under the heading, it is clear that God's message is to love Him with all that we are, to seek Him first, to come as He calls us, leaving all behind if that is what He asks of us, to love and serve Him by feeding His sheep and to read God's Word to renew our minds and be transformed instead of conforming to this secular world. To be a vessel of God's flame in motion, we must "test and approve what God's will is—His good, pleasing and perfect will" for our lives, and there is no better way than to search God's Word for ourselves and be transformed by His Holy Spirit.

Jesus is "the Way, the Truth, and the Life" (John 14:6). Renew your mind and find truth that sets you free while you are talking with God, listening to Him, and obeying His direction for your life. Anything God asks of you will align with His Word. If you choose to seek God and get understanding of the Bible, you can then shine His light for all to see. Along the way I learned, too, that if you agree with something spoken as truth, you can claim and declare it for your life. You can say, "Amen." Go ahead and say it out loud. No one is listening—well, no one except for God. You can smile. Who knows what great adventure He will take you on if only you are willing? Joy in the Lord always outshines the cost. His love in perspective always goes deeper and outweighs any sense of sacrifice. There is always the

joy of resurrection to any form of letting go, and it is the joy of
the Lord that is our strength as the heartaches we experience are
only fleeting moments compared to our eternity with the King
of kings. Follow Jesus and shine!

"This little light of mine, I'm gonna let it shine." These
lyrics (sung by Addison Road) keep playing through my mind.
This tune catches my attention every time it comes on the radio
or TV. If you do not already know it, I would love for you to
hear it! You can go to Addison Road's website and just soak it
in. Be still and at peace as you listen: http://www.godtube.com/
watch/?v=92MC91NU. I feel God's Holy Spirit all over me as
I soak Him in while I listen to this song. I hear the lyrics about
fire and *hope*. Jesus!

Wow! I know I need to finish this writing, but God! You will
make up the time if I just stop and soak you in and commune
with You, God! I need You, Lord. I need Your strength. I need
Your guidance. I need Your words. I need Your anointing flowing
through me. Most of all I am Your child, and I need Your love,
so open my heart Lord, and let me receive. I want to do nothing
else right now but receive You and respond to you with praise
and worship, for You are awesome and mighty and Your love is
powerful! Praise You, God! I praise You and exalt You! I lift You
high because that is Your place. You are high and lifted up! Jesus!
Holy Spirit, You are certainly welcome to take over this writing!
"Love in perspective?" It is Your love that matters. This writing is
all about inviting You to open our hearts and pour Your love in!
Now that's perspective! Praise God! Pour Yourself in that we may
pour out Your love to others! I love You, Lord! I love You with
everything in me, and I want this writing to be Your everlasting,
overflowing love in perspective! It is Your love and Your light in
us that pours forth that matters most of all! Lord, shine Your light
in the dark places of our soul. Fill the hurting places with Your

light and love! Let Your joy be our strength as we shine forth for You each day! Jesus! I need to stop and pray. Pray in Your prayer language or just talk with God. I am going to take Communion with Jesus, remembering His body broken for me because it is this simple and this powerful: "For God so loved the world that He gave His only begotten Son that whosoever believeth in Him shall not perish, but have eternal life" (John 3:16). "This little light of mine, I'm gonna let it shine." You are so childlike, so simple, and yet so brilliant God! Praise You, Lord!

If you have received Jesus as your Lord and Savior and have some juice and bread and want to commune with me and Jesus, just stop and take the time to do that now. Ask God to forgive you in areas of your life where you need Him and to help you forgive others who have hurt you. We do have to get into God's Word and shine the light of His truths on our souls, but right now it is all about simply stopping and seeking God with all your heart and loving Him because He first loved you! It is about His presence. He is present even if you cannot feel Him. He is present, and He wants a relationship with you! Just talk to Him and praise Him! Tell Him what is in your heart whatever is there. A relationship goes two ways. There is no such thing as a one-sided relationship. He wants to speak to you and share His secrets, and He wants you to trust Him with your secrets as well. He knows them anyway. Talk with Jesus. Precious child of God, listen for His heart of love beating for you!

Lord, this Communion bread is broken in remembrance of Your body, which was broken for the forgiveness of my sins. I take this bread, eat it, and do this in remembrance of You. Lord, this juice represents Your blood that was shed for me and for the forgiveness of my sins. Forgive me, Lord, even now for any place that I have fallen short and missed the mark, for any words spoken, wrong attitudes or behaviors that have grieved Your Holy Spirit and hurt those with whom I only want to share your love. Lord, as I drink the juice, I remember that by your stripes, that by those thirty-nine stripes of blood for the beating that You took for me I am healed. Lord, I remember that each stripe represents the thirty-nine sources of disease there are present, and so through You, Lord, I can be totally healed and whole in Jesus' name. Thank you, Lord!

Lord, I thank you for doctors and medicine and for all of the ways You choose to bring healing. I think of Delia, who was healed at the Bay of the Holy Spirit revival in Alabama, and how she was ready to leave there in her wheelchair, tired of being poked and prodded over the years with good-intentioned ministers of the Word, seeking for You to heal her. During other times I saw and heard her beautifully proclaiming Your glory and letting Your light shine through her many times on the platform, committing her life and love to You and proclaiming that You are holy to the world while spinning herself around in that wheelchair. There she was that August evening in 2010 after she had been physically bound in that wheelchair for more than twenty-two years. That night I felt something so powerful as I was sitting at my desk, and I proclaimed that You were doing something powerful to someone somewhere. I began praying and praising You. Then I saw the recordings on Facebook. There on the video, I saw Delia standing ... and then walking. Praise God! What God had done made international headlines, and one man spoke out from the pulpit a prophetic word for the church, "The bride of Christ is back on her feet again!" Hallelujah! Love in perspective! You are a God that saves! You are a God that heals! You are a God that loves us! We are vessels of Your love and Your light. We bear witness to the testimony of Your goodness and grace. We give You all the praise as we humble ourselves to be Your flame in motion on the earth today! Praise God!

One day at my New York church when I was still living in the area, I was praying, and God showed me a vision of Delia stepping out of her wheelchair and walking down that church aisle near where my spiritual mom, dear Wanda, usually sits. All to God's glory, others would be healed as well. I saw that day come into the natural. I saw with my eyes what God had shown me in my spirit. He showed me that there would be more people coming out of wheelchairs, and I believe Him. That day at the revival Delia was ready to leave when a baby who needed healing caught her attention. In her compassion, Delia stayed to pray for that baby. As she poured out compassion in her heart of prayers for the baby, God had her called to the platform, and that day, she stood and started to walk for the first time in nearly twenty-three years! I had seen her being wheeled around by Pastor Tommy and Wanda on our church cruise to the Bahamas a couple of years earlier, and here she was at the revival ... *walking!*

Lord, she took her eyes off her circumstances and put them on You with a heart for that baby, a heart of compassion that came from knowing You and Your love and compassion for us. Lord, by Your shed blood, if we confess our sins by faith, we are forgiven. Jesus, by the stripes on Your back, the beating You took for us, we are healed. I hope I never forget the prophetic word spoken for all of us in light of Delia's healing. I apologize for not remembering who spoke the words; however, they are still powerful, and so I repeat them to you, "The bride of Christ is back on her feet again!" What a *love story!*

Now, Lord, I can finish writing this chapter with love in perspective. Your love came first. You are our first love. We love because You first loved us. From there, Lord, we can let Your love and light shine to others as we seek Your guidance and walk in the light You shine through us. Your light shines on each step we take on the path You have mapped out for us. Your light causes us to shine like stars in the universe. Though Satan would love to snuff it out and does his best to hold us down and keep us back, it is all about You and all because of You that I can still sing my childhood song, "This little light of mine, I'm gonna let it shine, let it shine, let it shine—"

How can this be, though? Not everyone chooses God's light and love. How He longs to gather us *all* together and how He cries when He loses even just one of His children. The Holy Spirit grieves within me as I write, and I feel Jesus' tears in my own eyes. Jesus said, "Suffer the little children come unto me." We grow up and become the suffering little children innocently locked away in adult bodies with adult decisions to make. Jesus, do we choose you?

I cannot talk about "love in perspective" without mentioning that our God is both loving and just. There is a heaven and a hell, and I am thankful not to be the judge. In Paul's letter to the Roman church, he wrote,

> The wrath of God is being revealed from heaven against all the godlessness and wickedness of men who suppress the truth by their wickedness, since what may be known about God is plain to them, because God has made it plain to them. For since the creation of the world God's invisible qualities—His eternal power and divine nature—have been clearly seen, being understood from what has been made, so that men are without excuse. For although they knew God, they neither glorified Him as God nor gave thanks to Him; but their thinking became futile and their foolish hearts were darkened. Although they claimed to be wise, they became

fools and exchanged the glory of the immortal God for images made to look like mortal man and birds and animals and reptiles. Therefore, God gave them over in the sinful desires of their hearts to sexual impurity for the degrading of their bodies with one another. They exchanged the truth of God for a lie, and worshiped and served created things rather than the Creator— who is forever praised. Amen. Because of this, God gave them over to shameful lusts. Even their women exchanged natural relations for unnatural ones. In the same way the men also abandoned natural relations with women and were inflamed with lust for one another. Men committed indecent acts with other men, and received in themselves the due penalty for their perversion. Furthermore, since they did not think it worthwhile to retain the knowledge of God, He gave them over to a depraved mind, to do what ought not to be done. They have become filled with every kind of wickedness, evil, greed and depravity. They are full of envy, murder, strife, deceit and malice. They are gossips, slanderers, God-haters, insolent, arrogant and boastful; they invent ways of doing evil; they disobey their parents; they are senseless, faithless, heartless, ruthless. Although they know God's righteous decree that those who do such things deserve death, they not only continue to do these very things but also approve of those who practice them. You, therefore, have no excuse, you who pass judgment on someone else, for at whatever point you judge the other, you are condemning yourself, because you who pass judgment do the same thing ... God's judgment against those who do such things is based on truth. (Romans 1:18–2:2 LAB)

What a hard word from Paul in Romans when we think of a loving, healing God, but God uses these words as a ruler along with the help of His Holy Spirit to deliver us from the slavery of sin. We choose His way because God loves us and we love Him and want to live our lives in the ways He has designed for us. We choose God's "beyond anything we could hope or imagination" plans and purposes for our lives because God's love is so good that we want to obey and glorify Him. God is both loving and just. Otherwise He would simply be watching us destroy ourselves and one another with consequence after consequence of our actions. Our thoughts lead to actions. That is why it is so necessary to read the Bible and apply God's truths to our lives.

There are those people who seek God in their lives and then take God's love out of perspective and say things like this: "God is love, and so He may say we loved well when we love whoever and however we want." Remember Solomon? Read in 1 Kings how Solomon asked God for wisdom and followed the way of his father, King David, in obedience to God and in supporting every detail God gave him in regards to building the temple. Everything was dedicated to the Lord. Then King Solomon commanded that the Ark of the Covenant to be placed "in the inner sanctuary of the temple, the Most Holy Place" (1 King 8:6 LAB). God's glory filled the temple of the Lord. Praise was given to God, who consecrated the temple in His name, and then God spoke a word to Solomon about how he should not serve false gods. But Solomon strayed:

King Solomon Loved many foreign women besides Pharaoh's daughter ... These women who became Solomon's wives were from nations about which the Lord told the Israelites, "You must not intermarry with them, because they will surely turn your hearts after their gods." Nevertheless, Solomon held fast to them in LOVE. ... So, Solomon did evil in the eyes of the Lord. ... Although God had forbidden Solomon to follow other gods, Solomon did not keep the Lord's command. So The Lord said to Solomon, "Since this is your attitude and you have not kept my covenant and my decrees, which I commanded you, I will most certainly tear the kingdom away from you and give it to one of your subordinates. Nevertheless, for the sake of David your father, I will not do it during your lifetime. I will tear it out of the hand of your son. Yet I will not tear the whole kingdom from him, but will give him one tribe for the sake of David my servant and for the sake of Jerusalem, which I have chosen." (1 Kings 11:1–13 LAB)

We cannot solely depend on the lie from the father of lies that it is okay to love for the sake of love and that it is pleasing to God in all circumstances. Otherwise, God would be against Himself and His own Word. People taint innocent love while insisting on love's innocence. God is good! He loves us and wants the best for us just like any loving father would. Look at 1 Kings 2.

When the time drew near for David to die, he gave a charge to Solomon his son. "I am about to go the way of all the earth, so be strong, show yourself a man, and observe what the Lord your God requires: Walk in His ways, and keep His decrees and commands, his laws and requirements, as written in the Law of Moses, so that you may prosper in all you do and wherever you go, and that the Lord may keep His promise to me: If your descendants watch how they live, and if they walk faithfully before me with all their heart and soul, you will never fail to have a man on the throne of Israel."

From out of that promise, Jesus eventually came to earth in God's plan of redemption to reconcile us back to Himself through grace by faith. Even with God's perfect plan of redemption, we still have to choose His ways.

Blessed is the man who does not walk in the counsel of the wicked or stand in the way of sinners or sit in the seat of mockers. But his delight is in the law of the Lord, and on his law he meditates day and night. He is like a tree planted by streams of water which yields its fruit in season and whose leaf does not wither. Whatever he does prospers. ... for the Lord watches over the way of the righteous, but the way of the wicked will perish. (Psalm 1 LAB)

In the days of Solomon the Lord had him build a temple to house the Ark of the Covenant. In New Testament times God gave us a New Covenant through the shed blood of Jesus, the resurrected Christ. In Christ we are not free to "love" whoever we want however we want. We who have received Jesus as our Lord and Savior house the Holy Spirit. We are new creatures in Christ. Therefore, the Bible says, "Flee from sexual immorality. All other sins a man commits is outside his body, but he who sins sexually sins against his own body. Do you not know that your body is a temple of the Holy Spirit, who is in you, whom you have received from God? You are not your own; you were bought with a price. Therefore honor God with your body" (1 Corinthians 6:18–20 LAB). Once again, this is "love in perspective."

Biblical truths are not always easy to digest. Rather God's truths are straight and to the point. "The word of God is living and active. Sharper than any double-edged sword, it penetrates even to the dividing soul and spirit, joints and marrow; it judges the thoughts and attitudes of the heart. Nothing in all creation is hidden from God's sight. Everything is uncovered and laid bare before the eyes of him to whom we must give account" (Hebrews 4:12–13 LAB).

Why after such a refreshing time of writing does God have me stop and write out so much Scripture? I am not looking for or needing more material, and we all really need to search the Scriptures for ourselves to see what truths God has for us each day of our lives. The reason is that it is God's truth that sets us free!

When Jesus came as a little babe in the manger and then went on to die for our sins so that we may be reconciled with the Father (if we so choose), we received a new spirit and righteousness in God through Christ. Jesus overcame sin and death. When we get to heaven, we will have our new glorified bodies. For now, we have a soul of mind, will, and emotions that gets fed all kinds of wrong thinking in our world. Because of all the worldly thought that we could embrace as truth, we must feed ourselves the Word of God, the Lord's truths. Andrew Wommack has an insightful book out about walking in the Holy Spirit titled *Spirit, Soul &*

Body. I recommend his book for a clearer understanding of how the state of our soul affects the state and well-being of our lives.

To look at love in perspective of how God wants to love and show love through us, I also recommend books regarding boundaries by Henry Cloud and John Townsend. They have written books together and separately, such as *Boundaries, Hiding from Love, Boundaries for Kids, Beyond Boundaries: Learning to Trust Again in Relationships,* among others. The perspective God has given us in the chapter regarding love and the recommended books on boundaries really offer both perspective and balance in loving each other in God's way.

To offer yet greater balance and perspective regarding love, I lovingly finish this chapter with these words: "Even though we speak like this, dear friends, we are confident of better things in your case—things that accompany salvation. God is not unjust; He will not forget the work and the love you have shown Him as you have helped His people and continue to help them" (Hebrews 6:9–10 LAB). Take heart, be encouraged, and take time to rest in God's perfect love. Seeking, serving, and loving God as well as loving others in perspective is all about balance of God's truth and His presence. "This little light of mine, I'm gonna let it shine, let it shine, let it shine, let it shine. Won't let Satan blow it out. No, I'm gonna let it shine, let it shine, let it shine." Jesus! Glory to God in the highest!

CHAPTER 6

The Missing Foundation in American Higher Education

Jesus replied, "If anyone loves me, he will obey my teaching."
—John 14:23a LAB

Sentiment brings with it many memories of my college days earning my associate and bachelor's degrees in psychology and then securing my master's degree in student personnel administration. In everything I did, I tried to seek God, and sometimes what I was learning challenged me because the lessons went against the grain of my biblical beliefs. This process often lacked grace because I was earning the credentials necessary to work in the world, but I was forced to hold tightly to the tree of life and cling to God's truths. The key question is this: How do we ground ourselves when we are "in the world, but not of the world?" How do we ground ourselves if we have not spent the time with God in order to have the Bible as the foundation of His wisdom and truth? That is actually a good question, and I had so much more to learn spiritually (and still do). We all do.

There was one particularly unforgettable moment at the community college. While I was sitting on a hillside, talking with a friend, and taking in the view of the rolling hills and beautiful sky surrounding us, I sensed God telling me that I was a part of something big. It was something that I may never fully know, and rather than feeling grand, I felt my smallness in the scheme of things. I felt humble. I felt like a clumsy ballerina just trying to do the right things while keeping a smile on my face, sometimes succeeding well and other times simply fumbling and tripping myself up, but it has all worked out just fine overall with life sometimes getting in the way and sometimes making a way with pain, joy, sadness, loss, and always victory in the ways that matter most. I have had a long way to travel from childhood to my college days to the Bible school where my spirit leapt with joy of truths shared. I no longer had to go against the grain, but I could simply align myself with God's truths. He has been good and faithful to stay with me, and so I reflect on the work I have done, the mistakes I have made, and the grace God covers me with as I think about all the times and all the ways I sought diligently to include Him in my writings and my education.

Some may wonder, "Why is including God in higher education so important?" Every person who is educated on a professional level influences the area of expertise they are in, which includes the educational system at all levels and age groups (such as our children, grandchildren, and young adults who are leaving home and open to new environments), the business realm, the marketplace, the military, the media, the government, and so on, including the administration of our churches and even the degree of God's truths and flow of the Holy Spirit in our congregations, which are made up of people from all fields of employment. Please keep this rippling effect of national and international influence in mind as you read through this chapter. How are we all being affected by intellect and human understanding that appears factual yet is often void of the truth of God found in His Word, the Bible, and Jesus?!

James Robison and Jay Richards write in their book, *Indivisible*,

> The purpose of education has always been two-fold: to teach and to enculturate. Education should guide children to the Good, the True, and the Beautiful. It should enlarge their minds and their souls. It should provide them not only with knowledge, but with wisdom and virtue. It should help them find not just their calling, but their purpose. Unfortunately, secularism, relativism, cultural decay, a government near-monopoly over education, and educational theories that divorce socialization from the pursuit of truth have conspired to make a mess of American primary and secondary education. Some are skeptical that anything can be done. (Robison and Richards, 136)

Robison and Richards share the root cause leading to the Free Schools Act of 1867 and Oregon's 1922 Compulsory Education Act, which forced students to attend public schools. As for colleges and universities, Robison and Richards state that in the United States, "Students can get a terrific education. At the same time, modern colleges and universities (including some Christian ones) are often unsanitary brothels of bad ideas that can poison minds and spirits" In their chapter titled "Train up a Child in the Way He Should Go," they assert that "if you send your child to a public school ... you have to supplement their education if you want them to see how God and their faith are relevant to all those subjects they studied in school. Help them connect the dots during the normal years, and perhaps consider giving them a 'thirteenth year' after they graduate from high school, where you devise a curriculum designed to help them prepare for life and for college."

How can each of us individually and as a community of believers shine the light of Christ from within us in a world that relies on human knowledge, research, and norms of various moral and immoral reasoning, rationalization, and self-justification rather than knowledge and wisdom from the Maker of heaven and earth and the Creator of all of us as flames in motion and kingdom builders? As we pray and commit to living out "The Lord's Prayer," how will we shine God's truth in our world today? "Our Father in heaven, hallowed be Your name. Your kingdom come, Your will be done in earth as it is in heaven . . . ." (Matthew 6:9, 10 LAB)

Let us pray: Lord, we are earthen vessels in a big world. Shine your light through us and let your kingdom come and your will be done, all to your glory. I pray in Jesus name, amen.

I wrote the following self-analysis paper in September 2002 while I was working on my master's degree, and it is an example of my focus on God throughout my education. The question in light of supporting student development at the college/university level is the following: How does this student define the term "development?"

Here's my response: Development is a progression of assimilating consciously or unconsciously selected information from others and from the environment surrounding this student. This information touches and is influenced by the past, present, and future, which in turn touches and further influences the whole person. Development includes wearing all that is taken in so that this student becomes all that he or she is at any given time—with the goal of becoming the best that I can be. On one level, one can seek out development; however, on another level, development takes its own course. Development in this student's life comes as doors open, and I personally believe that God is ultimately in control of the open doors. Of course, He has a plan for each student willing to walk in obedience and faith. Development is challenging with obstacles, opportunities, breakthroughs, and blessings along the way. Further, development is like a math problem that one can sometimes solve easily and sometimes not; however, when one finds the answer, it all suddenly seems easy—that is, until it is time for the next "problem to be solved." In life, there is always another level to guide, develop, and better each of us as we confront what is before us. In a few words, development is the process of becoming who we already are.

There are millions of factors influencing this student's personal level of development. To begin with, there is God, others, and the self. There is gender, race, culture, nature, spiritual beliefs, differences and similarities in human beings, and the developmental progress of the entire world that connects and interacts with the uniqueness of this student. Some specific examples include growing up the only female with six brothers in a predominantly white, lower-class neighborhood, with two parents (later divorced), a maternal role model who succeeded in formal education through eleventh grade and remained mostly unemployed, and a paternal influence who worked in a factory and who was a self-taught guitarist that gave lessons on the weekends. Along with that brief description of influential factors, there are other factors, such as school curricula, professors, and being a married woman and mother returning to college as a nontraditional 1980s student in a society where the women's movement had come along and gender roles were being redefined.

One of the first papers this student ever wrote was called "The Stresses of Women in Transition."

This student has made progress academically and through work experience in my chosen field. The contributing factors to success include walking through the doors as they opened. Often, there was not a sense of being grounded, but there was one of continuing forward anyway. A desire for spiritual obedience has been crucial. God provides all that is needed for each step in each person's journey. Therefore; certain intelligence and abilities have been given to this student. Also, role models and mentors have been vital as far back as this student can recall. There has always been someone to admire, to interact with, to receive hope and encouragement from, to learn from, to soak in goodness, love, and positive regard from, to soak in something that said "keep going" even during the times this student felt like giving up. A contributing factor to this student's development was the ability to savor much out of every little bit.

Referring to a few teachers, there is the one who taught me sixth-grade music, and this person has remained my friend for more than forty years. There is the one who taught me undergraduate psychology and continues to be my mentor and friend since the early 1990s. (This touches me tearfully as she has since past away.) There are others (with and without professional titles of the teacher role) who made room and allowed me to talk about my deepest secrets and heartaches while I cried in their arms. There are the ones who traveled in their journeys, who overcame and succeeded in various ways in their own lives, who knew how not to stay stuck and somehow took this student of life with them through and beyond the areas of being personally stuck. These are my teachers of life.

Along the way I found Bible verses and promises to ground me as a student. They provide the true buried treasures in contributing to this student's development as well as prayer to overcome, to keep focus, and to keep going—even to write this paper.

As a final contributing factor has been, God keeps taking the bad stuff and turning it into something positive. However, we must ask this question: What factors have held this student back developmentally?

As a student, I wondered, *Am I really held back by anything in my development, or am I right on God's perfect schedule for my life?* There is this sense that there are temporary moments of delay, temporary moments of feeling hurt, discouraged, lost, afraid, and frustrated often because limitations imposed on the person by the self or others. There are also other priorities in regards to personal resources like time and money. Family is an important factor in the distribution of those resources—not because of what others say regarding gender differences but because family brings its own fulfillment and joy. Family offers its own rewards even while it appears to possibly stunt the developmental progress of what higher education has to offer—yet there is still a beneficial occurrence of development within the institution known as family.

Along with these beliefs there is still that one person who touched all of the right places inside this student. I had almost let this one person single-handedly destroy all of my hopes and dreams, all of the purpose planned within the field chosen by both of us. It took more than ten years to heal the damaged places and learn how to overcome through the counselor of counselors and those others God has placed in my life along the way. He has kept His promise to make good, and He has been faithful in doing so through the writings and my deeper development.

In answering the above questions, there seems to be some light shed that it is faith in God that brought this student through to graduate school and beyond. As for this developmental assessment; if a seat-of-the-pants approach works, maybe it is not such a seat-of-the-pants approach after all. Maybe it is a mix of theorist's theories already combined with this student's unique style. Maybe in some less organized fashion, the "informal theory" paradoxically offers some brilliantly organized theory of its own. Either way, there's more development to come.

Here is another sample of including God and my faith walk in my academic experience:

In Student Affairs, we have focused on the importance of considering the student as a whole person with unique intellectual, emotional, physical, social, vocational, moral, religious, and economic backgrounds and differences (SPPV). The RESPECTFUL model (D'Andrea & Daniels, 1997; 2001) addresses human diversity at a time when multiculturalism is a priority in higher education and society overall.

R—religious/spiritual identity

E—economic class background

S—sexual identity

P—psychological maturity

E—ethnic/racial identity

C—chronological/developmental challenges

T—various forms of trauma and threats to well-being

F—family background and history

U—unique physical characteristics

L—location of residence and language differences

This model is taken from Allen E. Ivey, Michael D'Andrea, Mary Bradford Ivey, Lynn Simek-Morgan in their *Theories of Counseling and Psychotherapy; A Multicultural Perspective*, 5th edition textbook. They introduce the RESPECTFUL model as a "comprehensive model of human diversity that has practical utility for the work of mental health professionals" This model gave me a lot of mileage in sharing my faith as I focused on "R," religious/spiritual identity. One thing I have learned more clearly since my graduate school days is that our identity is in Christ and who He says we are in His Word. God will always be developing who I was born to be as I keep my eyes on Him and allow my heavenly father to transform me throughout life. I fully believe that my developmental process using the RESPECTFUL model significantly reflects that I am further along in life through faith than a model without a faith focus would indicate.

The following thoughts are adapted from an article critique regarding multicultural awareness. It was written in 2003 for one of my Student Personnel Administration classes. For the purposes of this book, *Flame in Motion*, I am not including an article specific to the following reaction. My present day goal is to share ethnic diversity as it relates to faith, the manifestation of good versus evil and how I respond to these multicultural challenges from a faith perspective. While my insights at the time of this writing revolve around the disarmament by Saddam Hussein of Iraq, the current relevancy could be applied to any system of disunity including an international perspective or perhaps student personnel challenges at an urban college campus. I do not see myself as a political person or one very well versed in what is going on in the political front, but I would recommend keeping our eyes on God in relationship to Israel during any season of unrest.

Communication by educated representatives of diverse backgrounds throughout the world has not been able to unite

the nations or prevent evil actions. There are those who would view disunity as a lack of multicultural acceptance. Still others would call it a prophetic battle of end times. Either way, wars have continued, our young men and women have been killed and we are all affected by our differences from international governments to college campuses.

As for ethnic diversity there is the biblical story about the tower of Babel in Genesis 11 LAB. The story begins, "Now the whole world had one language and a common speech" (Genesis 11:1). Then the people united to build a tower to make a name for themselves, thereby putting themselves above God. To stop the building of this tower, "the Lord confused the language of the whole world. From there the Lord scattered them over the face of the whole earth" (Genesis 11:9). Believing God's Word, we will come together again the way we were separated through the living God. Those things in the Bible that God considers sin will remain sin-related rather than diversity-related even while we were all created equal under one God, with "one language and a common speech." Whether the issue of diversity involves war for religious freedom or deliberate immersion of students into unfamiliar cultures with a goal of embracing diversity; God is greater than us and the various levels of battles that we face.

Given the multicultural, political, and spiritual times, this critique scratches only the surface of what is present and is to come. From a Christian viewpoint, we are one in the Lord through the power of the risen Christ. As for the sin and evil within this world that tries to sneak its way in on the heels of multiculturalism, victory has already been won.

The move to embrace differences while we remain strong in our uniqueness is a sign of the times. Textbook readings in the field of counseling and also in areas of student personnel administration include exercises and applications regarding multicultural beliefs, awareness, and practices. Before one even gets started with the chapters in *Theories of Counseling and Psychotherapy: A Multicultural Perspective*, Ivey, D'Andrea, Ivey, and Simek-Morgan introduce the RESPECTFUL model as a "comprehensive model of human diversity that has practical utility for the work of mental health professionals" (Ivey et al., 2002). As for diversity, the Bible prophetically tells of a time when there will be "a great multitude that no one could count, from every nation, tribe, people and language, standing before the throne and in front of the Lamb" (Revelation 7:9 LAB). In a Bible study workbook and video *Beloved Disciple: The Life and Ministry of John*, Beth Moore describes this multicultural gathering as "the consummation of perfect unity in glorious diversity" (Moore, 179).

On a national scale of multicultural differences, a war began the very evening of my class paper (March 19, 2003). In the March 2003 issue of *TIME* magazine, Howard Fineman quoted President Bush as telling religious broadcasters that "the terrorists hate the fact that we can worship the Almighty God the way that we see fit" and that the United States was to bring God's gift of liberty to "every human being in the world." Some would see Bush as "a man blinded by his beliefs." Others would see this act as a lack of multicultural acceptance. Still others would again call it a prophetic battle of end times. Ten years later, in a current example of terroristic acts against the United States based on multicultural differences, two words come to mind that touch us with great compassion for our country as being "one country, under God, indivisible" and those two words are "Boston Marathon." (We need to humbly stop and unite in prayer for our country.) "If my people, who are called by my name, will humble themselves and pray and seek my face and turn from their wicked ways, then will I hear from heaven and will forgive their sin and will heal their land." (2 Chronicles 7:14 LAB)

A professor shared an article with me on the topic of holy wars. This is the same professor who laughed about me publishing my first book and who called it *Vanity Fair*. I am thankful that he motivated me so that my first book, *Finding the Way*, did not sit in the basement and I would seek God's advice about how to promote and distribute more than two thousand copies nationally and internationally. Even now his laughter does not stop me but sparks a flame in me to write this book, *Flame in Motion*. With God, I do not have to worry about promotion and distribution today. We are not to despise small beginnings. I just have to do whatever is in my power to do and give God this writing and whatever else happens is up to Him as I give God all the glory. This is true for you in whatever He has called you to do as well. Anyhow, the following is my reply to the professor with his doctorate in psychology regarding the paper he sent:

I do not understand Holy Wars, but I know that on some levels, I have always been in one of my own for daring to have faith of any variety. Yet, in my world of faith, the picture looks nothing like any of these images in the expression of itself. I see myself in intimacy with the Creator, an intimacy that remains somehow childlike and innocent. I look at the suicide bomber and the vicar's (priest) son and see the difference rather than what is common. It appears the vicar's son has turned his nuclear disarmament campaign finally onto himself where he has disarmed his own interior nuclear defenses to see the simple meaning and rich purpose of his father's existence. Still, I understand perhaps the wiping of his brow with the sigh of relief, 'Phew, the suicide bomber could have been … anyone of us in our search for self and for our higher purpose.' 'And what exactly was the true calling upon the life of Judas?' I ask myself as an aside. I have had to grieve my own process of internal nuclear disarmament throughout the years, letting go of one defense strategy after the other from prior years of just trying to exist in the midst of freewill chaos and its more subtle terroristic destruction upon the human soul. How paradoxical to have to fight for peace. How naive to think we can live in this life of sin and free will without a battle—holy or unholy. We need to somehow end up with love in our hearts. Only in our hearts can there be an answer to the original question. What do a vicar's son and a suicide bomber have in common? It is all about what is in the heart. 'Man looks at outward appearance, but the Lord looks at the heart' (1 Samuel 16:7b LAB). God looks at our impurities only through the righteousness of Christ. Jesus said, 'I am the way, the truth and the life. *No one* comes to the Father except through me' (John 14:6). Our Father, God, sees the heart of righteousness through Jesus. God said to King David that the prophet Samuel had come looking to anoint the boy as the coming king of Israel. A small boy was to replace King Saul on the throne of Israel, and he was successful in many holy wars against giants who came against God and worshiped false gods in their own selfish agendas. David was not without sin, but he knew who to turn to and offer repentance. David was a man after God's own heart. Let not our love grow cold. Love for God because He first loved us and love for the Savior who came down through the generations from David's own seed is the difference between the suicide bomber and the vicar's son. Jesus, what, as my professor asked, do they have in common? We have in common the free will to choose Him. Take this moment and talk to Jesus. Receive His way, His truth, His life, and His love for eternity.

Professors and the institutes of higher education have a phenomenal amount of influence on our lives and communities, so I find it necessary to convey that these amazing institutions may pour out some facts based on research. However, you should be careful because facts are not necessarily truth, and listening to the majority in finding norms is not necessarily in alignment with God's truths. Then, in effect, we have generations of teachers, business people, and whoever else is influencing our society based on ideas, beliefs, and a literal effort to influence students and the world in ways that are not always God's ways. I am not interested in discerning the information that aligns itself with God's Word and that which does not because I have walked that road already. I just want to lovingly be on guard in my sense of discernment as to what I embrace as a practice or out of personal need. I need to be clear in knowing that God is first and watch out for anything that might lead us down a wrong path or make any type of institution or idea a false idol. Being in unity with a large group is not necessarily being in unity with God. There is a lot of pressure at times to fit into boxes of organized thought and theories made up by men and women with good intentions.

In the following excerpt from another one of my graduate papers, I want to share some of a three-part review I wrote regarding values, disciplinary counseling, and life's purpose. This presentation provides an overview of key challenges facing student affairs and higher education professionals. It also proposes that institutes of American Higher Education return to the foundation of whom they have been created—having originally been founded to educate clergy and promote the good news of Jesus Christ throughout America. (Wait a second. Did you know that about higher education having been originally founded to educate clergy? It is true that building many well-known and accredited institutions of higher education early on in American history was a faith walk made by some of the first leaders of this country to educate clergy in the new life where there was to be no holy wars, but to promote the saving grace of Jesus Christ throughout this great new country, the "home of the brave and the land of the free," the United States of America.)

There is so much literature that conveys important issues in addressing the needs of students in American higher education, yet most all of them politely avoid the use of Christianity, God, or any form of spirituality as a foundation for the questions they seek to answer. While student personnel administrators seek to teach a student personnel point of view for educating the whole student, the foundation of spiritual development is indeed the sole missing piece. The likes of Noah Porter (Yale) and James McCosh (Princeton) have been shut down in their 1880's efforts to keep the college a religious one, and all that remains from those early days of the emergence of the American university is the fact that the Christian voice appears to be the most oppressed voice of all across the board. These places have become widespread institutions of secular education. For whatever criticism is held against Laurence R. Veysey, author of *The Emergence of the American University* (1965); he is credited by this student for exposing the truth of what happened to this aspect of our existence with regard to the American colleges and universities.

The vast numbers of institutions of higher education are here largely because they were built on faith in God to educate clergy. Yet colleges and universities have disempowered themselves by removing the biblical truths that have held firm for thousands of years. Students are counted privileged to read textbooks and topics not grounded in biblical truths and wisdom. Those students who seek to fill the spiritual void are left to make the grade while they also need to bridge the gap within the mental, emotional, and spiritual realms of development. To those who have managed to hold onto biblical truths and remain within their relationship with God, there is always in every educational endeavor, an awareness of the void, no matter how sophisticated the literature is presented. As future staff within student affairs (and fellow Americans) we are left with the weight of finding solutions to issues that have been spinning in circles for centuries. Yet the battle is a greater one than any and all of us can fight alone, for the battle itself is a spiritual one of good and evil. We can do the work that is before us in obedience to God's purpose; but ultimately, we are not to shoulder this awesome responsibility because the battle belongs to God and He has already won the victory.

The victory in Christ means that it does not matter how it appeared when Noah Porter pounded his fists on the table after he was figuratively beaten down by the crowds. What matters is that Porter chose to fight the good fight and aimed wholeheartedly to keep religion in institutions of higher education. It also did not matter how it appeared when Jesus was nailed to and hanging on the cross. *Despite how it all looked, the Son still shines, and the Creator of all of life still reigns. And we are not Him.* God does not force Himself or biblical truths on anyone. The error of the early days of American higher education was that leaders made a huge mistake in their authoritarian style of Christian discipline and compulsory church attendance. They used this format as a way to help students improve upon their values and find their God-given purposes, yet human force in spiritual realms can only fail. Still, we do not dismiss the office of counseling from our educational systems when it does not serve to discipline misbehavior. Rather, we seek to learn how to best utilize this service for the good of all.

Why then have we thrown away the Christian basis of what our institutions could have offered us? Why have we diluted what we have been privileged to receive and offer our world? Why have we taken the foundation of our Christian beginnings and disposed of the good rather than improve upon our human errors with the help of God? Instead, we took our human errors and transferred their humanness onto God, who simply seeks to have a relationship with us so that we may love Him and love one another in this process of education known as life. We open our thoughts and our hearts by asking, "What kind of world do we want?" I, for one, know that I do not want a world without God intimately present in it and God at the foundation of everything.

I shiver as I feel God's power in these words. I remember reading them in my History of American Higher Education class and with that uncommon liberty came a warning following the reading. The professor graciously advised me to be careful to include all religions. Oh, flame in motion. God help us to shine your light and share your love everywhere we go.

CHAPTER 7

The Church

Come to me, all you who are weary and
burdened and I will give you rest.
—Matthew 11:28 LAB

There was a day when both of my parents took us to church. Just as quickly, it seemed, my father stopped going. My mother, a young wife with four small children, tried to go. I saw her stress. She stopped going to church. She sometimes dropped me off for Sunday school. Even at five years old, I found light in the midst of darkness, and I wanted to be there.

By age nine, three of my grandparents had died, and my best friend and my cousins had moved out of state. In my grief and sense of inadequacy I quit ballet and piano. I had lost interest. My dad paced behind me as I sat on the piano bench, and he yelled at me to practice. He slammed his belt on each side of the bench as he went by. He stopped to pound my back with his fist. He told me I was a quitter and had no backbone. I kept going to church.

At age ten a woman walked down the alley where I played with my friends. We were planning a carnival for muscular dystrophy. She asked us if we knew God as our personal friend. I wanted to understand what she was saying and to know more. She helped with the carnival and invited us to a revival. I received Jesus as my Lord and Savior.

Four years later my dad sexually abused me. I didn't know what to do, so I asked my grandma for her keys to the church and knelt at the Communion rail. In the quiet of the sanctuary, I cried to God and asked, "What do I do? Who do I tell?" I didn't feel that anyone could handle what I wanted to tell them, but mostly, I felt too ashamed. I kept going to church and joining in offering myself there however I could even while the shame grew and the secrets increased. As I reached out to God, I never quit.

Through the years people have made fun of me for my faith. I have messed up, and I have done well. There may be those who don't understand, those repulsed by their own sinfulness in light of my faith while they project their shame onto me, those Christians who think they are better than me, but all in all there is no one who can cause me to turn away from Him. He is Jesus.

There were times when I wanted to die and take my own life, but I never would. The spiritual oppression, the incest, and the criticism only cause me to want our heavenly Father all the more. Others may try to steal my innocence, my joy, my faith, my purpose, and my walk, but they will only push me closer to Jesus because I will never quit.

God shows me Himself in the awesome realm of His glory. In such a place not long ago He took me back to that church of my younger days. In my mind's eye I saw where I once knelt at that Communion rail. In the spirit, kneeling before Him in the sanctuary of a more recent church, He told me that I had come to the right place and met the right person back then. I had come to Him.

He is the One, faithful and true, always present all of these years, always guiding me, always opening doors. I am His child. I may not play piano or dance ballet, but in seeking Jesus, I will *never* quit! The beauty of it is, as He holds me in His arms, He loves me with an everlasting love. His love never fails, and I will never quit because He is faithful!

In a world of whatever all the challenges are that each of us face, I believe that the "gates of Hades will not prevail" against the church. Whatever the gathering of God's people mean to each of us in encouraging one another, we need the body of Christ to come together. These are tough times, and some of the world gets played out in the church; however, iron sharpens iron, and we are charged to continue to assemble, encourage, and love one another. For all of the imperfections that imperfect people bring into the church and all of the ways we hurt one another, I perceive and believe that there is still the light of Christ in the church as well as much more light in the world because of the people who make up the church and because they spread God's Word, the light of truth through Jesus, who is the light of the world.

The Word of the Lord will remain forever as the Bible declares, "For all men are like grass, and all their glory is like the flowers of the field; the grass withers and the flowers fall, but the word of the Lord stands forever" (1 Peter 1:24–5 LAB). In writing about the Word of the Lord standing forever and the gates of Hades not prevailing against the church, let us look at the church as a building and also as an ecclesia or a gathering of God's people wherever we are, whether at the city well in Old Testament times or at the marketplace in today's world. If all the church buildings in the world were destroyed (God forbid), those of us who have been made new creatures in Christ would still exist because we are the church. Look at China with its underground belief system. The pressure to prevent such a body of Christians from forming and growing only forced the "church" to grow all the more. Think of this reaction as one squeezing juice from grapes through a winepress to make fine wine. What people intended to be preventive only made the church more extensive. Why? Because the pressure in our lives, like in my personal life at times, only makes us need and appreciate the Good News of Jesus, His light, His love, and His salvation all the more. If all the church buildings in the world were brought down, every stone on the buildings that fell to the ground would still only prove to become stumbling blocks to those who do not believe. For those who do believe, these very stones would be stones of hope crying out the praises of glory unto the Lord. For those who do believe and those whose hearts are open to hear the stones' praises, they would be unable to keep themselves from joining in the sounds of joyful worship echoing through the heavens. Hallelujah!

What does Scripture say?

> As you come to (Jesus), the living Stone-rejected by men, but chosen by God and precious to Him— you also like living stones, are being built into a spiritual house to be a holy priesthood, offering spiritual sacrifices acceptable to God through Jesus Christ. For in Scripture it says: "See, I lay a stone in Zion, a chosen and precious cornerstone (Jesus), and the one who trusts in Him will never be put to shame." Now to you who believe, this stone is precious. But to those who do not believe, "the stone the builders rejected has become the capstone" and "a stone that causes men to stumble and a rock that makes them fall." They stumble because they disobey the message—which is

also what they were destined for. But you are a chosen people, a royal priesthood, a holy nation, a people belonging to God, that you may declare the praises of Him who called you out of darkness into His wonderful light. What else is God saying to us? Once you were not a people, but now you are the people of God; once you had not received mercy, but now you have received mercy. (1 Peter 2:4–10 LAB)

You should also consider the following: "You are no longer foreigners and aliens, but fellow citizens with God's people and members of God's household, built on the foundation of the apostles and prophets, with Christ Jesus Himself as the chief cornerstone. In Him, the whole building is joined together and rises to become a holy temple in the Lord. And in Him you too are being built together to become a dwelling in which God lives by His Spirit" (Ephesians: 2:19–22). "He (Jesus) is 'the stone you builders rejected, which has become the capstone.' Salvation is found in no one else, for there is no other name under heaven given to men by which we *must* be saved" (Acts 4:11–12 LAB).

And, there is more. "(Jesus) asked His disciples, 'Who do you say I am?' Simon Peter answered, 'You are the Christ, the Son of the living God.' Jesus replied, 'Blessed are you, Simon … you are Peter, and on this rock I will build my church, and the gates of Hades will not overcome it'" (Matthew 16:15–18 LAB). Therefore, "God so loved the world that He gave His one and only Son, that whoever believes in Him shall not perish but have eternal life" (John 3:16 LAB).

"Now that you have purified yourselves by obeying the truth so that you have sincere love for your brothers, love one another deeply from the heart. For you have been born again, not of perishable seed, but of imperishable, through the living and enduring word of God." (1 Peter 1:22–3 LAB)

Wow! See, I was telling the truth. In everyday language I was sharing the Word of God. *Jesus loves you!* Open your heart to Him and make Him Lord of your life today and forever, or you can recommit your life to Him. Find the promises that God has for you in His Word. Find a church that embraces the truths of God's Word. People sometimes hurt one another rather than show God's love, even in the church, but keep your eyes on your heavenly Father and remember that He built the church, which the gates of hell will never overcome. So never give up. Allow God to love you, especially in places where you hurt or have been misunderstood, and let His love flow through you. Be a holy vessel and allow the holy cornerstone to be your foundation wherever you are and wherever He leads you. He loves you with an everlasting love! Let His light shine through you! Amen.

I often think of how God led Noah to build the ark, the church boat that eventually housed the only followers of God on the earth at that time. Imagine how people probably laughed at, mocked, and criticized Noah, who certainly did not fit the norm and was likely considered as crazy as anyone is in our society today who does not fit the norm or fit in with the in-crowd. Imagine how when the rains began, Noah's family was safe on his boat in obedience to God and how good it probably felt when the breakthrough came and there was dry land again. Like Noah, we as the church are a peculiar people if we walk in alignment with God's will. How great it feels during those times we break out of the boat or out of whatever box we find ourselves in and step up to the plate of obedience to serve God however He asks. Whether out on the waters or on dry land, our feet are on solid ground with Jesus as our foundation.

A family member's funeral comes to mind when I think of stepping out of the box. I was in a room filled with many young people. There were all kinds of perceptions of God. Some lined up with the Bible, and some did not. There were those with drug addictions, family who were carriers of Christ in support of one another, Christians who came and stayed, and those who came and hurried on their way. There were those trying to seek and obey God wholeheartedly and others who said they loved Jesus but who did whatever they wanted. If only we could show our love to God by pleasing Him with the obedience He longs for so that our hearts can be fully open to His embrace. The pastor's message focused on "Let not your hearts be troubled" and included my nephew's poem of his personal relationship with God. There, in the midst of some obvious darkness in the room, was a strong spiritual heritage that went back generations. My nephew asked Jesus into his heart a week before he died. He prayed and wrote poetry about his thoughts of God long before that prayer of salvation. We have to believe that God will bring to completion the process He has begun. There I stood and related to others with love, hugs, and my bright Jesus pin that was shining like diamonds against my black pantsuit, the pin given to me by a dear friend from my New York church. I lit up when I opened it and took *Jesus* out of the box He had been packaged in because, as she said, "I knew you would love it because you love Jesus." Yes, I do love Jesus. I even love saying His name as I type it here—Jesus. To some, I may have looked like I had a religious spirit for wearing that pin—even around Christians and members of the church. To others who were visiting their handsome, young friend and loved one lying in his casket; I believe that somewhere inside of them, they were desperate for Jesus even if they did not know what they were desperate for. Could they look at the pin on my jacket shining in the darkness, hear my nephew's poem of God, hear the pastor's message, see the love, feel the Holy Spirit calling them, and connect it to Jesus. Would they then come to Him? God sees the heart. He knows if it is repentant and submissive to guidance and grace. I hope the seed planted through my nephew's life—literally having been placed in the ground that day—made a difference in the lives of those remaining and that others turned to Jesus for forgiveness and everlasting life. That gathering, though it was a funeral service in nature, was church. We were gathered together before God that day. Jesus—

There are other examples of people who stepped out of the box as Noah did, such as Joseph, who was thrown into the pit where he was left by his brothers to die and eventually made it to the palace where his brothers bowed down to him and received life-sustaining food; the shepherd boy, David, who had been prophesied to become king with jealous King Saul trying to kill him; and most importantly, Jesus, the carpenter's son who was crucified by the mobs only to be resurrected from the dead so that we could all have eternal life with Jesus. These lives show us a pattern of being in the world, but not of it. These men were thinking outside of the box where they were rejected to the point of fighting for their very lives. Eventually, they transcended the genuine attempts to be destroyed by those who did not have the mind of Christ. They broke out of the box and broke forth into the victory of all God had for them and for us who believe and keep our focus on Jesus. He is risen! Hallelujah!

I have two movies in mind: *Patch Adams* and *Dead Poets Society*. Patch says he is still there, a thorn in the medical establishment's side as he finds unconventional ways to reach and treat people. In *Dead Poets Society*, the boys stand on their desks and proclaim their uniqueness with "My captain, my captain" as they honor their teacher, who has to leave the school for daring to be different and stand for his beliefs. We have this glimmering flame of hope inside of us where we all get enthralled by this idea to step out of our boxes and comfort zones in life and seize the day (*carpe diem*). The enemy seeks to snuff that God-given spark out of us in whatever way he can and often through the people we love the most. To overcome with Christ, to step out of the boat and walk on water with Him is the reason why these movies and more current ones become so well known. We have it in us. We want to, but if our call is so big that we know we are unable to seize the day or the accomplishment, then we must fully rely on Jesus because "all things are possible with Jesus." His strength is actually made perfect in our weakness. *Patch Adams* did not fit in. The boys were afraid to stand against the oppression of who they were meant to be. Something rose up from within them like that which rose up in Joseph and King David, and that something is called purpose and faith. It's enough to move mountains.

There is a risk to be taken and vulnerability of being rejected when stepping out in faith to answer the call of God on our lives. Jesus was rejected. We need God's wisdom and guidance if we dare to step out of the box, to face those who would like to shut us down in whatever way, and to wait on God for the breakthrough so that we can break out in triumph as God leads us in His triumphant procession. God goes before us as we seek to love and touch other lives all to God's glory.

Church, we need to think out of the box, beyond rejection, beyond breakthrough to a year of breakout! Like the members of the "Dead Poets Society," we need to do what the teacher said. We need to be in a mode of carpe diem where we seize the day. We need to stand on the chair and look to our heavenly Father even when we are at most risk for rejection and call out to our Lord, who calls on us to not only think but step out of the box, *Jesus!* "My captain, my captain!"

We need to assemble together as the corporate body of Christ with a common purpose of loving God, loving one another, and taking the good news of God's love, salvation, reconciliation, and discipleship to a lost world. Key to moving mountains in Jesus name is becoming one body in unity with others in which all parts of the body are necessary to function to God's purposes and glory. Jesus prayed on our behalf, "Father, just as you are in me and I am in you, may they also be in us so that the world may believe that you have sent me ... May they be brought to complete unity to let the world know that you sent me and have loved them, even as you have loved me" (John 17:21b–23 LAB).

The hardest part about being corporate is when those in the body of Christ are attacking, backbiting, rejecting, competing, publicly condescending, and condemning others with their words. This is also present when they follow such condemnation by hiding behind the idea that we as Christians are not to take offense. Jesus did not come into the world to condemn the world and would not hide such behavior behind an additional criticism of not taking offense. This is hard for me because of both personal pain and the pain of seeing this creating disunity in the body as a whole. Like Jesus did with the money changers in the temple, I believe Jesus will turn the tables. I would hope to seek unity, and if that does not work, I would like to step back and believe that God will make good of those things men intend for evil. If the intentions are for good, God knows the heart, and so I would still step back and seek God to heal me and believe that He works all things together for good to those who love Him and are called according to His purpose. In either case, it is essential to focus on God's forgiveness for me and through me, and I need to walk by faith to pursue the plans and purposes He has for my life. If the situation was long-term and it caused tension, distress, and disunity in the body, I would go to someone in authority. At this point, I would have to let it go and let it be between me and God. Beyond my prayers, I would no longer be accountable other than to continue to seek unity, love, and peace as much as it depends upon me. We all sin and fall short of the glory of God, but by grace, we are saved.

God, help us choose to forgive. Help us where we fall short. Restore our relationship with You and others in Jesus' name so that we can give You glory because the more important thing is walking in the freedom that Christ gave to each of us when He died and was resurrected. We have been restored by our Lord. We can realize who we are in Him. Praise God when we come to that place of corporate unity as a church body! Glory to God for how powerful that unity is! How healing occurs! How the anointing breaks the yoke! God loves us too much to leave us where we are. Thank you, Jesus! Amen.

I have said that I sometimes need a break from structured religion to get my spiritual focus. I am not willing to give up on the church, but there are times when I have taken a break from it so that I could rest and refocus on God as the central reason to participate in a church family. It seems contradictory to take a spiritual retreat from church life, but Jesus left everyone to be alone in the garden of Gethsemane. I think there needs to be more emphasis on pastors having a place to get away and be with God without the demands of the congregation. How can they feed the flock if they have no food left to give? Church can be a tough place, and it is sometimes the place where spears are thrown. For whatever reason I think at least part of the stress is that people are seeking to relate on less superficial and professional levels and more as families with whatever dynamics each person brings. I have felt in need of healing at times from trying to love and having my weaknesses shoved in my face as my hand is reaching out to help. I have loved taking time to soak in the presence of

God at conferences with missionaries who made light of how the path of the Western church has diverged from God's. I have skipped conference sessions that had any person trying to give all the answers to being a better Christian because I could not cope with anything in my mind beyond just being in an atmosphere of Christ's love. I have laughed hysterically at the humor of what we make it, and I have cried at the pain and exhaustion I felt from my experiences. People prayed for me as well. Strangers who are my friends, my sisters, and my brothers hugged and loved me when I needed love and healing. It is okay if you need to let go for a moment with you and God. He is still holding you. He is faithful not to let you go. He knows when you need a rest, and He knows your heart for Him even when you are resting. Maybe it is okay to be still and know that God is God and the battle belongs to Him ... if only we take the steps that He lights for us as we take each step at His pace, an often slower and steadier pace than the world would have us believe. Sitting at Jesus feet, washing them with my tears, and drying them with my hair sounds good to me, and that is exactly what I need sometimes because you don't know the cost I have paid in my life and in my walk with Jesus or the price that Jesus paid to save me in the intricacies of my life.

A friend avoided me for a while and then eventually wrote the following in a letter to me:

> I lost my sense that I had anything to say or could find a way to say it and began to question whether God had really given me any kind of mission or that if he had, I could ever hope to fulfill it. Although I still love God and Scripture, and wish things were different (about the world, about me), I finally felt I had to take a break from the church and my deep aspirations to find a personal

expression of faith that would sustain me or help others, and simply see if I could rebuild myself or figure out my direction better when the daily pain of confronting my own expectations and hopes and their contrast with the reality I faced in church and elsewhere had become less of a gaping wound and less of a constant source of shame and anger for me.

I believe this decision represented a loss of confidence on my part, but it was the best I could do ("just as I am, without one plea")—I just didn't have any more fight or sense of spiritual purpose in me. I was driving myself crazy and feeling angrier and stressed out *all the time* because I just couldn't accept or get past the expectations or the sense of their absolute futility. After about a year of being away from the church (and by the way, no one knocked on my door or called me to encourage my return; instead, my absence, and my efforts to express the unhappiness I'd felt were totally unimportant to anyone, as far as I could see, further validating my sense of utter futility), I began to feel less angry and sad and more "normal," and occasionally, even eager to find something different than the church I'd attended, so I could try to reestablish my relationship with God on a basis other than "what is it you want me to do for you?" which I felt I'd either botched or totally misperceived earlier. I'd begun to hope that my "descent" had been something I could learn to better understand and write about from a spiritual and scriptural viewpoint, although I certainly had no clear sense of whether I'd be up to the task. At best, I'd noticed how, after working so hard, when my adult spiritual journey began in the 1970s, to get in touch with the sweet and loving spirit within me that longed for and drew strength from direct contact with God, something in me had shut down again over the subsequent years and was more like Elijah's whisper than the roar of the wind or the crash of the thunder. I don't consider myself the same as I was before the 1970s but definitely in a different place spiritually than I was, say, ten years ago, or even in 1998.

I longed to still be able to enter deeply into God's presence in prayer and sometimes feel *certain* of what God's will for me or someone else was, as I often had in those long-ago days. I'd come to feel that my experiences with a rather unresponsive and unloving mother had made it much harder for me to get in touch with Mary (or the spiritual mother within me) than it had ever been to get in touch with the child betrayed and misused by a male representative of the church. And so I had my work cut out for me, I felt, even if I didn't know that it would lead to any writing or ministry per se. After a long period of feeling exhausted and passed over like busy Martha, I'd hoped to sit at Jesus' feet and see what I could still learn. In essence, I felt that letting go a couple of years ago was letting go of so many hopes and dreams related to a sense of closeness with God, all of which originated early in my childhood. I'd come to feel that letting go was necessary and possibly even good for me, at least compared to what I'd been doing to myself by continuing to hold on—that letting go was an adult response instead of the more needy and desperate response of a child longing for love and attention who refuses to ever let go, since she feels she will lose everything if she does. And although I'd like to have had whatever it took to hold on longer, I know that I still don't have it. I'd begun to suspect that, somehow, the brokenness in me, the inability to hold on after a long, long time of continuing to try, and losing my grip a little more after each heartbreak or setback; the determination to hold on because I'd come to hope against hope that things would work out as I'd originally imagined them, instead of letting God really call the shots—that particular adaptation, which essentially describes my entire life—can be traced back to my sexual abuse by a minister of the church, but was first set in motion, as it were, by my troubled relationship with my mother (and various substitutes). Although I don't blame myself for what happened with my abuser or my mother, I don't think I would have been nearly as susceptible to his attention, or felt as devastated by his post-abuse rejection if I'd had a loving relationship with my mother (or found the way in the ensuing years to heal that loss).

As I read about my friend's spiritual experience, I felt compassion for her, and so I wanted to understand her heart as I read more of her words. She continued with the following:

Oh, I could detail some of the things that especially got me down about my efforts within the church, especially the church of my adult years. But I came to see that these gaps I'd struggled with for so long are not the ones felt by adults who simply find religious practice or personal wanting; they are a reflection of the crushing of an innocent child's spiritual trust and goodness, when she first looks to church leaders for guidance and role modeling of the faith journey (and redemption from an absence of maternal love). Can male ministers really "get it" when a female tries to share her heart, without getting hung up in their own sexual or rescue fantasies? And I have reflected on all these things and more, over the past couple of years and even before. Still, by the time I took a break from the church, I'd come to feel not only that my own expectations were the driving force behind much of my own disappointment and misery, but that what I needed from the church was fairly unique to me and inspired by my early wounding, not something I was likely to find in a regular church setting. Once I came to that view, it just seemed pointless to continue to get more and more "evidence" of what I felt I needed but almost never received—my disappointing experiences had become a mirror to my soul but not a mirror to God or to my path of healing. There are only so many people one can talk with about the deepest of one's fears and longings and feelings, and I certainly count you as someone who would surely understand. But, while I do share your sense that love and God are ultimately more healing than psychological theory or treatment, I probably have a different sense of the church than you, and possibly a different sense of where we are in our respective personal or spiritual journeys.

That was my friend's heart that she shared with me, a place in her life that God was bringing her through. I am sure that she shared these thoughts and feelings in prayer with God and that He was faithful not to leave her or forsake her. In response I know I was searching my own heart and seeking God in the following reply to my dear friend:

Jesus loves you as a separate and precious being in your own right and always has. Even when you could not feel His love coming through your mother in the way that you needed, deserved and were worthy of having just for being alive, God made you and He wonderfully formed you in your mother's womb. She didn't understand that you were formed there for God's purposes and not for her purposes or to be an extension of your mother or who she needed you to be. I'm sorry for how she made you feel and the consequences while also believing that God will not let any of it become wasted even when we cannot always see or know His higher purposes.

In looking at those things in life that have shaped the person I am today, I remember a time when I was six years old and climbed the huge tree in the corner of our yard. I climbed out on the limbs and onto the roof of the neighbor's garage. I did not know how I was going to get down. My mom and neighbor came outside to see the situation I had gotten myself into. My mother called out, "You got yourself up there, now you can get yourself down." It's an interesting dilemma when the tree limbs I stepped off of as I secured myself on the garage roof were unstable to grab hold of for climbing back into the tree. That was my only way of getting down. I thought my mom must have surely been very old and unable to be up there with me, get me down, and help support me from a place closer to the trunk of the tree. When I look back, I realize that she was not old at all. She was only twenty-eight, and a friend watching on with her was only in her early twenties. At fifty-three, I would still give my best effort to climb the tree for my grandchildren, but I guess it was a life lesson meant for me to learn about being out on the limb on my own. It is funny how that works because my mother inadvertently taught me how important it was to do these things on my own when she did not help me.

My friend later again wrote to me,

> Do I really have something of God's own heart to offer others What keeps me going is the great joy I get from engaging with Scripture and trying to articulate some of what it means to me; and from striving to live with faith by carrying out all that faithful living means, making use of the particular playing field and the particular resources I've been given. I strive to embrace life with both courage and humility, but it's hard to feel so isolated and ineffectual in the process.

Here's my reply to this precious friend:

With words that expose secret places that no one wants to talk about (childhood sexual abuse) with the hope of helping, I live in the shadows of those millions of things spoken to tickle people's ears. I live in the shadows with what too many people don't understand, yet I love in the light and with the light of God; that is, I hope to love with God's light at least in my graceful moments. I smile, laugh, and play so as not to waste words on people who would only trample them. Large pink elephants in rooms surrounded by people who act like the elephants aren't there. I look to do what is in my hand at the particular given moment and to be attentive that God lights every step of the way. I desire to please Him. I am surrounded by people who love me, yet it is "hard to feel so isolated and ineffectual in the process" of walking out my faith and God's purpose for me. Between these moments of reading, typing and tears, I think about starving children, missionaries isolated in far-off lands, and soldiers who give their lives. During these thoughts, I am thankful to be me ... not really so isolated, not really so alone out on the tree limb or on the roof where they watch to see how I'm going to get down (or if I will make it back to having both feet on the ground, as if that is a firmer foundation). What is the greater good of God's ways that are higher than our ways? Love?

Another friend who was crying during our prayer time shared good news with me. Her husband had a breakthrough regarding their daughter having been molested as a child by the elder in the church. Rather than me going with her to talk to the pastor, her husband went. The conversation was successful. The pastor is taking positive action to confront the situation. I wonder how many others could step forward and how God will heal them. I pray that the barriers of silence are broken. We'll see what God continues to unfold. Sometimes I feel like my book (*Finding the Way*) didn't do much even though, like with the little drummer boy, it was my best to give. Hearing how this woman believes there has been a turnaround and hearing her thank me for beginning the new thing, after so many years of struggling and being immobile with what they knew, helps me to see light in what I offered— that limb I stepped out on to let my testimony of incest and God help someone else.

My friend encouraged me by writing, "Don't give up all the things you have fought so hard to defend and articulate over the past few years—there are many ways the forces of evil and diminishment cast their shadow over our lives; only God can keep us in the light of His peace and acceptance."

I replied with the following:

It is refreshing to simply bow my heart before God in prayer, praise, and worship. I love to lose myself and soak in His sweet presence. At times, I simply feel used and empty. I can't fool you that I have something to give because I have nothing to offer other than to meet you in the acknowledgment of God the Father, Son, and Holy Spirit as Healer, Savior, Provider, Comforter, Father, Friend. When broken and there is nothing there, He is. Surrender it all to God and find rest in Him, but don't give up. I know you are tired. I'm tired. We all are at times. I don't blame any of us if we want to give up, but don't. God is with us and working for my good in some way, whether or not I see it.

She then gave me some sweet words (and I think provided a message for her own heart as well):

My only simple advice is to continue to pray and be clear about your own needs and feelings, even if others disagree with them or do not seem to fully accept them. In the meantime, I pray that God will comfort and direct you on your journey, helping all concerned align their hearts to Jesus' own instead of mistaking their own agendas for God's will.

My friend returned to church and more fully reached out to God and His love in her life. I eventually ended up in Bible school after one of her last messages to me before she died. She wanted me to set boundaries in my giving to others because she loved me and wanted me to take care of myself, too. In the messages we shared and that "last supper" we ate together, we had church, and God was surely with us. "In his heart a man plans his course, but the LORD determines his steps" (Proverbs 16:9 NIV).

Heavenly Father, thank You for Your truth that sets us free. Bless those who seek to love You with all their hearts, souls, and minds and to love others as themselves. Heavenly Father, forgive us when we fall short. Forgive us when we do not love others as ourselves or lay our lives down for one another. Forgive us, Lord, when we hurt and disappoint You by hurting and disappointing one another because we have fallen short of your greatest commandment. Forgive us, Lord, when we blame others for our inadequacies and self-imposed limitations. Forgive us, Lord, when we place one another in boxes of misperceptions and misjudgments that cause all of us to receive less than all that You have for us. Forgive us for oppressing one another and feeling justified with our blind rationalizations. Forgive us when we join together with others in misunderstanding and lack of knowledge to make false judgments about Your children. Forgive us when we crucify You through one another. Thank you for forgiving us when we know not what we do. Help us to know what we do, Lord. Forgive us for judging and calling brothers and sisters out of the very boxes that we continue to put them in. Have mercy on us when we think that we are doing this in love. Forgive me, Jesus, when I have done this. Forgive us, Lord, for the moments when we are not walking in love and freedom and when we impede the progress of others as well. Lord, forgive us when we do this in Your holy name and speak out to others as if the message is coming from Your own lips. Lord, in Your holy name, I break off the boxes, like prison walls and chains on slaves, and say, "Let my people go. Let my people go! Let my people go!" Free them, Lord, in Jesus' name and to Your glory that they may continue doing the work of Your kingdom that is present and is to come. Free us, Lord, so that we may continue to walk with You in the power of Your resurrected life and in the victory that You have given us. Almighty God, may this prayer be the iron that sharpens

FLAME IN MOTION

iron as we seek wholeheartedly to love and serve You and to love
one another as ourselves. Thank You, Lord. Praise You, Father.

We must always ground ourselves by standing on God's Word:
"Therefore put on the full armor of God, so that when the day
of evil comes, you may be able to stand your ground, and after
you have done everything, to stand. Stand firm then" (Ephesians
6:13–14a, LAB). And, "Shout for joy, O heavens; rejoice O earth;
burst into song, O mountains! For the Lord comforts His people
and will have compassion on His afflicted ones. But Zion said,
'The Lord has forsaken me, the Lord has forgotten me. Can a
mother forget the baby at her breast and have no compassion on
the child she has borne? Though she may forget, I will not forget
you. See, I have engraved you on the palms of my hands'" (Isaiah
49:13–16a LAB).

Church family, the best thing to do with all of these issues
we face in our houses of God is to truly set all personal agendas
aside and press in corporately with totally abandoned praise and
worship of God. Pastors and worship leaders, I have seen God
breaking yokes and setting captives free. Bringing unity is best
done when pressing into the worship without time restraints and
ritual while still maintaining an orderly flow of service. Following
the Holy Spirit and allowing God to open our hearts to His felt
presence is best when we wait upon the Lord in our songs and
prayers of praise and invite Him to lift us on eagle's wings. Best is
when we allow one another to be both doers of God's Word and
also careful to take those times to rest in our freedom to rest in
Jesus … to be still and take His peace upon ourselves and listen to
His love for us, His song singing over us. God inhabits our praises!
How beautiful and powerful His miracles, signs, and wonders
are and how sweet smelling His fragrances are when we abandon
ourselves to Jesus in uninhibited ways. At a concert recently all of
the people in the front of the room were abandoning themselves

in their love, movement, praise, and worship, and everyone around me toward the back were seemingly frozen, as if moving or breathing would embarrass them or dishonor God. Do we have the courage to breakout and not be embarrassed or ashamed of the glory of the Lord and to sing out praises to Him? What are we afraid of? To lose control is to gain control. What corporate unity we could have and share together if we were to let go and let God run our services! I have seen so much contrast in our churches, but this is my cry to the Lord: "Lord! Please don't ever let me fall asleep or have to worship with those who are asleep because I so love you and your felt presence!" "Shout for joy, O heavens; rejoice O earth; burst into song, O mountains! For the Lord comforts His people and will have compassion on His afflicted ones" (Isaiah 49:13).

Regarding the functioning of the church, in his book *Apostles, Prophets and the Coming Moves of God*, Dr. Bill Hamon focuses on prophets and apostles being restored back into Christ's church, united as part of the fivefold ministry in preparation for the second coming of Jesus, and how these fivefold ministries will function interdependently. What is the fivefold ministry? It is where God has called some to be pastors, some teachers, others evangelists, and others to be prophets and apostles. God's kingdom is being established in our lives and in the church as discussed also in Myles Munroe's book, *Kingdom Principles*. Dr. Hamon describes what is happening is that holiness and righteousness are being laid to God's plumb line. God is separating the wheat from the chaff. He is purifying the prophets, apostles, and the church body for His purposes. Dr. Hamon prophesies, "Now is the time of God's people camping around the Mountain of God until everyone knows his or her calling, placement, ministry and relationship to God's greater purpose within His local and universal Church." The Holy Spirit is taking us into the "Apostolic Movement and final restoration moves of God." National and international "ministries are being brought forth," and man-made traditions are being removed. The role of "pastor" will be (and is being) redefined. "The Apostolic Reformation" will make church leaders and pastors more committed to raising up an army of equipped saints than an audience of paying spectators and fans." Dr. Hamon states, "Many leaders will not be able to make the transition because of their fear of losing control or lessening their authoritative position."

I cannot think of apostolic studies without thinking of my New York pastor, Bishop Tommy Reid, who always has close to his heart the desire to be in the heartbeat of what God is doing. I consider him to be an apostolic father and leader who promotes networking and unity. He also helped establish COVnet, an international network of networks. Tommy Reid has connected people over several decades for the sake of the kingdom in fulfilling God's purposes and by having many known and unknown ministries branch out from His leadership. To me, Bishop Reid has been a forerunner as an Apostolic Father and leader, and he has also remained a humble man who has stayed faithful to seeking and promoting the good news of Jesus Christ around the world. I never wanted to leave Pennsylvania, but I am thankful that God allowed me to witness His presence and His moves for five years in my New York church family, the Tabernacle.

Dr. Hamon writes of several more coming moves of God, but to me, the interesting thing is that the apostolic movement will prepare the way for the saints' movement. Apostles and prophets will arise "in the world of administration and finances ... and God is preparing an apostolic and prophetic company of Christian business people" who will "affect the economy in many nations of the world." Saints will be trained up and equipped to go out and compel people to come into the kingdom of God with supernatural ministry of the Holy Spirit.

Saints are being trained up in schools throughout the world today, including Bible schools that focus on the presence and power of the Holy Spirit in our lives. For me, I look at what God is doing in these times with marketplace ministry, and I see how He has taken my husband's field of geospatial services and has allowed me to share the work God has had for me, my book, *Finding the Way*—the way being Jesus as the way, the truth, and the life—with some of his colleagues locally and nationally. That is marketplace ministry, and on some small level, it is in alignment with the saints movement, for we are carriers of God's light just by showing up in the marketplace.

I see and appreciate each of our unique gifting even as we are all made in the image of God. For years, I've been saying to myself and to others, "Do what is in your hand to do." We do not have to fit into someone else's idea of what we are to do or be. If we do what is in our hand, God can bring us together to glorify Him and fulfill His purposes in a way that we cannot orchestrate ourselves or even imagine.

I remember being at a church service, watching two people praising and worshiping in the Holy Spirit. I noticed that both had their eyes closed and that they were moving their bodies and arms about so gracefully. What amazed me was that they were side by side, and while their arms were moving in dancelike motions to their sides and into one another's personal space, they never touched or bumped into one another. They did not know this was happening because their eyes were closed, but God opened my eyes and led me to watch. On a natural level they did not always see eye to eye, but spiritually, it did not matter. God had a plan and purpose for each of their lives, and whatever their peculiarities were in the natural world, God was showing me how they flowed together in His Holy Spirit. God brought that unity to the forefront of what He was doing in that church. He was demonstrating His Word, "Not by might, nor by power, but by my Spirit says the Lord Almighty." (Zechariah 4:6) Those two people flowing in the Holy Spirit during praise and worship (with whatever their personal differences were) represent how the fivefold ministry and the saints movement are to flow together. Through surrendering our wills in spiritual unity and because of the power of God's Holy Spirit, we shine forth His light to a dark world.

God told me in the late 90s that I had a lot to learn but that He would be with me through the process. He told me in the 80s that I was a part of something bigger than me, and so by the late 90s after I had learned a lot of things the hard way, I asked God to take my will and make it His will. He helped me publish a book, and now I have distributed over two thousand copies. As for the saints movement that Dr. Hamon describes, I feel that we who belong to God and who are seeking His will in our daily lives are a part of that movement to equip the saints. I believe that we all have much to learn and that as we continue staying in the process of transformation that God has for us from the time of our calling to our commissioning, we will continue to be vessels of the supernatural power of God's Holy Spirit. We will often flow in His Holy Spirit as a natural part of our seeking Him and allowing His light to shine through us. I believe that we will flow in what He has called each of us to do and that we will produce a rippling effect reaching out to other church bodies, not by forcing our beliefs onto anyone but by simply being contagious carriers of God's Holy Spirit. I want to continue to press into my relationship with our loving God and move forward in His plans and purposes while I remember that no matter what, He is victorious, Jesus is coming back for His bride, and all we have to do is what is in our power to do—simple and challenging all at once. Just trust and obey, and you will see that God will work all things together for good to those who love Him and who are called according to His purpose. If we each simply do what is in our power to accomplish and contribute to the benefit of one another, God will bring it all together. After all, our heavenly Father has each of us in the palm of His hand, and He will also do what is in His hand to do. He'll bring the rest of His moves into being, and He will use what is in His hand, you and me, to fulfill our callings if we so choose to do His will. We are and continue to be His flame in motion. So, Lord, thy kingdom come, thy will be done. Whatever God has for us, remember this most of all: Take time to simply breathe and rest in Jesus because resting in His arms and listening to His heartbeat is the best place of all. Be still, Church, and know that He is God.

CHAPTER 8

Walking in Victory

No one will be able to stand up against you all the days of your life.
As I was with Moses, so I will be with you. I will never leave you
nor forsake you. Be strong and courageous because you will lead these
people to inherit the land I swore to their forefathers to give them.
—Joshua 1:5–9 LAB

On December 20, 2010, Dr. Mark Chironna wrote these words on Facebook: "There comes a moment in your journey where going inward takes precedence over what you previously accomplished to prove yourself to others. The shift that marks this compelling decision involves leaving the known for the unknown, the radical search for your unique life's dream. No one can make that journey with you and some may choose to disconnect from you; while others seek to prevent you from making the shift."

On December 22, 2010, Mark Chironna wrote, "You arrived here already called. You have had to embark on a quest to come to know it. Lifelong learning, a willingness to grow and develop, and a readiness to abandon inadequate models of reality that cannot support that call, are part of your process. The most important aspect of this call is your connection to the still small voice within that is guiding your footsteps. That connection connects you to all things."

I missed Dr. Chironna's Facebook status between December 22, 2010 and October 2012 because I began living his timely prophetic words. "where going inward takes precedence over what you previously accomplished to prove yourself to others." I seemed to disappear into another place or way of living, and I had rarely been online to keep up with Facebook friends, even though I did care about them.

All in all I feel like I have been on a mission from God. Wherever I have lived (I have moved many times) and wherever I have gone (I have traveled quite a bit), I have found myself caring for people and addressing needs on all levels of spirit, soul, and body. I do all I can with Christ in me to be the hope of glory that God calls me to be. There is nothing fruitful that I do to my credit. Anything good comes from the Holy Spirit in me. I love God because He first loved me, and I seek to do his will no matter how clumsy I may be at times. God made me and gave me this heart of compassion, and I have almost always—at least as long as I can remember—been in a role of ministering to others who hurt by listening to their felt needs and offering encouragement and whatever spiritual truths I knew through God's Word and prayers. Over the past two years there has been a change where my focus became my husband, daughters, and grandchildren along with Bible school and my new family in the Lord. Since I graduated with my ministry license, my focus has been even more centered on those closest to me and relating to others in more social ways through the church, the Internet, and hopefully this writing. It has been a season of learning how to set new boundaries and pointing others to God. That does not mean that I stop praying for people or listening and caring. It means that it is all about what

God can do, even if He does it through me from time to time, whether I even know He is working through me or not.

I find this new season to be a healthy change for me. I became tired of living in other people's choices and going around the same mountains with them living in their consequences, carrying burdens while some continue doing what they want to do often apart from God's will. I want to have fun. I want off that merry-go-round that causes my head to spin and my stomach to be sick. I have a heart for everyone, but it is not by power or might but by God's spirit. If His strength is made perfect in my weakness, then I do not have to be a martyr. I especially do not want to keep people stuck because I am enabling them somehow. I do not want to keep myself stuck this way. I want to walk in the victory that is already mine ... the victory that is already all of ours through Jesus!

For example, I no longer want to walk with men and women in their forties, fifties, or older who do what they want all week and show up to church at some point. Am I supposed to think this is some kind of great accomplishment? I am sure people feel this way about me sometimes as well, maybe that I need to grow up, but it is time to focus on the younger generations and not those living in worldly ways who are in my age group or older, people who do not want to lay down whatever is holding them back in the Lord to grow up in Him. I want to shake loose and have God help me maintain the good boundaries He has taught me through my classes in Bible school. That does not mean that I do not want to help where God calls me or do what He tells me, but I do not want to go around in circles with anyone. God died so that I could have freedom. I want the joy of the Lord without others trying to rob me of it. I want to relax or enjoy things with my husband, children, and grandchildren without interference. I want to focus on God, write books, and ride my new Honda scooter that I have wanted since I was a child. This is my life, and I have been through some hard things even recently; however, I want to play Ping-Pong with my husband and walk the beach with him and play with our grandchildren, Skylar and Nathan, and spend time with our daughters, Julie and Heather. I want to press into my loving relationship with Jesus and worship Him wherever I am and wherever He takes me. I want to do what God has for me, and I know that He wants me to walk in His victory. I love everyone, so whoever is with me is with me and whoever is not is not; however, God will never leave me or forsake me. I know that much from a lifetime of believing and counting on Him, and He is faithful.

I have at times been told that I am a pastor, and I received my ministry license in 2012. God has closely connected me to a multitude of pastors and pastors' wives through the years. God told me in 2006 when I moved back to Pennsylvania from New York that I would be a friend to many churches even as I so longed to plant myself and find my church family comfortably and securely within one church building. In June of 2012 God moved us, and we reconnected with the church that we were members of before we moved to New York in 1998/1999. Since around 2009, Greater Works Bible School was the closest I had come to settling in with church family, and it was still not that foundation of family within a church building sharing the routine experience of Sunday morning worship I wanted to count on. While I was in Bible school, I lived an hour and twenty minutes away. I lived in a beautiful new home God had given us on top of a mountain that made winter driving especially challenging. Everywhere I went around me was down a snow-covered mountain, even when the terrain at the bottom was often clear. Still, I have loved God and others enough to walk the extra mile and to be a Good Samaritan and help someone in need. I have walked in faith to share biblical truths despite the possible consequences. I am not always the most graceful in the steps I take and the things I offer. I have a lot to learn, and I am always seeking to learn more; however, my heart for God is to cultivate His peace and love wherever I am, even when it means I have to go to battle or remember to rest in God's loving care because the battle belongs to Him.

Christ's resurrection gives us victory wherever we are and whatever we are doing. Sometimes it looks like we lost the battle like when Jesus was nailed to the cross, beaten, and bloodied beyond recognition, but not so! Jesus did what was in His power to do. He fulfilled His purpose here on earth and spoke out for all of us that "it is finished!"

Throughout His three-year ministry, Jesus healed the sick, cast out demons, gathered and taught disciples, established His kingdom here on earth, broke bread and gave Communion, held others close to Him, washed feet, and did all of the other things written in the Bible, and even more accounts of His life and ministry than books of the Bible could ever begin to tell us His full purpose. In all of these things, He had human emotions and wilderness experiences. Then the time came, and what was in Jesus' power to accomplish? His arms were stretched out on that wooden cross, and nails pierced His flesh, holding our precious Lord and Savior in place as nonbelievers mocked and humiliated him. That was what was in Jesus' power to do. He who knew no sin was crucified, dead, and buried for our sins. He was born to die for us, but however bleak that existence appeared, it was not the end of the story. On the third day, He arose! What was in His power to accomplish here on earth? He arose, and like Joshua leading the people into the Promised Land, Jesus has a Promised Land for those who believe!

"Though the doors were locked, Jesus came among them and said, 'Peace be with you!' Then He said to Thomas, 'Put your finger here; see my hands. Reach out your hand and put it in my side. Stop doubting and believe.' Thomas said to Him, 'My Lord and my God!' Then Jesus told Him, 'Because you have seen me, you have believed; blessed are those who have not seen and yet have believed'" (John 20:26b–29 LAB). We have overcome the challenge by the words of our testimony and the blood of the Lamb. "He who has an ear let him hear what the Spirit says to the churches, 'To him who overcomes I will give the right to eat from the tree of life which is in the Paradise of God'" (Revelation 2:7b LAB). We are the righteousness of God in Christ. God help us to know who we are and walk in victory with Jesus! Help us to know our identity in Christ and to seek to be more like Him that we may be carriers of His Holy Spirit and go light our world! Help us to be the flames in motion that we are meant to be! Praise you, Almighty God! Amen!

CHAPTER 9

Pray for the Peace of Jerusalem

Though the doors were locked, Jesus came among
them and said, "Peace be with you!"
—John 20:26b LAB

God is so awesome and so worthy of praise. He redeemed the people of Israel from Egypt and set the prophetic truths in every detail throughout the Old Testament to tell of the coming Christ of the New Testament. God performed miracles and drove out the nations and gods that stood in the way. Nothing was going to stop the coming of the Messiah, which had already been set in motion. God made the people of Israel His very own forever and made a way to also redeem us from our Egypt (this world) so that we could also be God's own people forever. In wanting us and the intimacy of relationship with us, He made a way for us to be His people and for Himself to be our God forever. The way is Jesus! Hallelujah!

We do not know the hour of His return, but Jesus is coming again. In Isaiah 62, Isaiah prays persistently for the salvation of his people. "For Zion's sake, I will not keep silent, for Jerusalem's sake I will not remain quiet, till her righteousness shines out like the dawn, her salvation like a blazing torch … The Lord has made proclamation to the ends of the earth: 'Say to the Daughter of Zion, See your Savior comes'" (Isaiah 62:1, 11 LAB).

Would you like to know a mystery? This mystery has been kept hidden for ages and generations. It is a mystery that I know about because it has been disclosed to the saints. Who are the saints? The saints are those who believe that Jesus is the Messiah who has come out of God's love to reconcile us to the Father and give us eternal life. Paul reveals this mystery to the church, "To them God has made known among the Gentiles the glorious riches of this mystery, which is Christ in you, the hope of glory" (Colossians 1:27 LAB).

God gave Paul a commission to present the Word of God in its fullness. With Christ in us, we are the hope of glory to those who are lost and dying in our world. God has destined our purposes in life down through the ages and generations—primarily that we share the full gospel throughout the ends of the earth and make disciples of everyone. God makes a point to note family heritage throughout the Bible and show how we all connect in the plans and purposes of God.

Like a mother who gives birth to a baby full of life and potential, a baby with plans set forth by God before conception, we do not know what is being delivered through us. We only know that we have a choice to say *yes* and seek God's plans for our lives and simply wake up each day and do what is in our power to do and always ask for more of God, for more of our heavenly Father, for more of His love and His life through us, for more of His felt presence, for more of His mercy and grace, for more of His fruit to manifest in our lives, for more of His light to shine on each step of our way, for more of Him, for more of our roots in Him, and for more of our Daddy, Abba, Father.

After I spent all night researching my heritage, I began to ask God why knowing the foundation of my heritage was so important. While I wondered if I was wasting my time, I began to realize how important my (and all of our) heritage is. A couple days later, I was in bed and nonchalantly asked God what He had for me to write in this section with the chapter title He gave me, "Pray for the Peace of Jerusalem." The next day, I received an e-mail to watch *3DWoman* on TCT online. A loving and passionately creative speaker and worship leader from my New York church, Pastor Aimee Sych is one of the hosts. I also watched several segments of *Living Epistles*, hosted by her phenomenal yet humble father, Bishop Tommy Reid. All of the broadcasts are excellent, but one segment I almost missed suddenly caught my attention and became of great interest to me.

Jeremiah 31 talks about the descendants of Israel. God speaks of His everlasting love for the people of Israel and basically says that He will be their God and that they will be His people. Our heritage and roots are Israel. As long as the world exists, the descendants of Israel will live. It is a covenant between them and God. We pray for the peace of Jerusalem. Through covenant, God has established His name in Jerusalem. Robert Stearns on *Living Epistles* as interviewed by Bishop Tommy Reid says,

> We need to do more praying. ... If we look at the scriptural mandate, Psalm 122:6 NRSV, "Pray for the peace of Jerusalem, they will prosper who love thee," something happens in our hearts when we pray. It begins to inform our priorities. It begins to inform our value system. ... Begin with biblical obedience. ... Pray for the peace of Jerusalem which is the city of the coming of our great King. ... Covenantly, God has established

His name, he says, in Jerusalem. Pastor, God has linked His reputation to what is going to happen in the city of Jerusalem. He says, that in the last days Jerusalem will be established as the mountain of mountains, the city of cities, and all nations will stream up to worship the Lord in Jerusalem. Certainly, we know that won't come in its fullness until we see the coming of the Messiah, but we can begin now to turn the compass of our heart to the city both of our spiritual birth and the city of our hope which is the city of Jerusalem and pray for Jew, for Arab, for Muslim that God's plan will invade the failings of man. Pastor, this is a mess (recorded in 2010 and compare even today with what is going on and current news only increases our need for prayer and peace according to God's plans). The Middle East situation is so fraught with pain and anguish and difficulty. It will take a Heavenly answer to come to that part of the world and bring peace and hope.

Bishop Reid declared in summation, "And definitively, God wants us to pray for the peace of Jerusalem."

"Okay," Bishop Reid continued, "let's take this one more place. I sat as a child and heard about the fact that Israel was going to become a nation—1930s. I saw that happen. God's doing something special in the Middle East, isn't He? In spite of all that we have heard on television, there is another agenda for God, isn't there?"

Robert Stearns replied, "Pastor; we live in a momentous time in history. God has fulfilled His word to His people Israel and regathered them in the land. The Bible says Jerusalem will be trodden under by the Gentiles until the times of the Gentiles are fulfilled. Jerusalem once again was unified in 1967. We're living in a strategic moment in time and I believe every Bible believing Christian must begin to turn their heart in prayer towards God's purposes for His city."

Tommy Reid then said, "Just in closing, the Bible gives us the ten commandments. The first commandment is to honor God. The last six commandments are to honor other men ... Is it important to honor our forefathers, the Jewish people?"

Robert Stearn replied, "One of the last verses, if not the last verse of the Old Testament says that the Lord will turn the hearts of the fathers to their children and the hearts of the children to their fathers. Could it be that in this day, God is taking the Gentile church that sprang forth from Israel and is turning our hearts toward them. And could it be that at the same time, God will turn the hearts of His ancient people Israel to the church and God's plans and thoughts will be higher than we ever imagined?" Tommy Reid said, "I believe that" (Trinity Christian Television, Living Epistles show 522, 2010).

God is setting up seers in the church, and we see that with revelation there come responsibilities. Our characters must be able to uphold the amount of power we carry, or else we become dangers to those around us. We are vessels, and God does the rest. Do what God says and step away. Put responsibility back on Him. *Unity* will come when we all know who we are in Christ. When Jew and Gentile become one, we will really see God's power. Pray for the peace of Jerusalem, the Messiah's return, and worldwide revival. We are a part of God's eternal plan. Jonathan Welton in his book, *The School of the Seers,* writes, "Discerning of spirits is always hand in hand with love! The restoration of discerning of spirits is the final bridge to the movement of love and unity in the church." We are one with God. We are "His bride, His people, and His church" (Welton, 183, 185). We are the expression of God's love. It is a new day to walk in His love.

As I think about our heritage in Christ and the purposes God has for us, we each have something in us that wonders why we are here. Esther, a young Jewish woman, became the Persian queen to King Xerxes. She courageously went to the king on behalf of her people even though she could have been killed. Esther was born "for such a time as this," and a whole nation was saved because of what she did.

When I learned more about praying for the peace of Jerusalem, I had been looking into my heritage, and I discovered that, along with Harry S. Truman, Dick Cheney, Barack Obama, Gabriel Duvall, Bessie Windsor, Betty Duvall, Robert Duvall, and Warren Buffett (http://www.geni.com/projects/Descendants-of-Mareen-Duvall-of-Middle-Plantation), I am also a descendant of the French Huguenot and early American settler named Mareen Duvall (1625–99). Huguenots were Protestants who left France because of religious persecution. Apparently, Duvall did very well on his plantation in Maryland. His granddaughter, Elizabeth, married Dr. William Denune, also a Huguenot, who "came to Maryland after 1721, shortly after he graduated from medical school in Paris" (www.denune.org/). I believe that the Denunes had economic and political influence going back to Scotland during the 1200's and that Dr. Denune was a likely match for his bride from the successful Duvall family. It is uncertain if Mr. William Denune, a minister for 19 years in Pencaitland in East Lothian, Scotland was the father of Dr. William Denune. Minister William Denune married Isabella Hepburn, who was the daughter of Dr. George Hepburn. Dr. Denune and wife, Elizabeth Duvall, had a daughter, Jane Denune, who married Vachel Howard, and they named their son Denune Howard. This name has been passed down through the centuries so that my grandfather, his father, and his grandfather kept this name, Denune. My brother's middle name is Denune, and he gave his son the middle name Denune as well. The name goes back through the generations at least to Dr. Denune in the early 1700s. "Denune" is a Scottish name. (http://www.denune.org/pdf/obama.pdf).

For me, there seems to be something there in my heritage— some connection that I feel inside of me knowing that God set all this in place for His purposes. I do appreciate a possible connection to ministry that goes back to the 1600's in the Denune family. While I am very interested in my heritage, I do not usually read all of the relationships that detail who begot who in the Bible. Someone once did, though, and out of it came a little book that likely made millions and more importantly, touched millions of lives for God. The book is titled *The Prayer of Jabez* by Bruce Wilkinson, and it was published by Mulnomah in 2000. This *New York Times* best seller was about "breaking through to the Blessed Life" based on 1 Chronicles 4:9 and 10. Jabez prayed, and God answered his prayer in the chronicled context of who begot who, which I always skipped over because it was boring to me. In my family, Denune Howard (1757–1842) married Anne Anderson and had Absalom (1780–1843). Absalom Howard married Mary Smith, and they had Nancy (1804–95), who died in Dunbar, Fayette Co, PA (where I lived when I was born). Nancy Howard married a man named Miner/Minor in 1821 who died young. She married again to Simeon Provance in 1833. She had Denune N. Provance (1838–1913). Denune N. married Mariah Coleman in 1859, and they had Denune J. who died in 1922. Denune J Provance married Catherine Cummins in 1887 and they had Denune Elias (1901–70). Denune Elias Provance married Jeanette Marie (Nettie) McNair in 1918 (my Grandpap and Grandma Ned as I called them). The Denune name skipped my father, but my grandmother related to my mother that the family name had always been important through the generations. (Maybe someday God will reveal some treasure or trinket of information as to why it is meaningful. For now, I am content knowing there are Scottish origins and a tie to the Stewart family also of Scottish origins such as a tie between me, my husband and our early paternal heritages and we are here, for such a time as this, to glorify God through this book and through whatever way God calls us to bring glory to Him!) My brother and his son received Denune as a middle name. To date (May 2013), the name Denune has not yet been passed down in this generation of children (another reason I am recording it in *Flame in Motion*), yet it clearly shows a tie to such earlier generations and the Duvall genealogy.

More important than those family ties and whoever I am distantly related to, Acts 3:25 LAB documents God's covenant word to Abraham, "You are heirs of the prophets and of the covenant God made with your fathers. He *(God) said to Abraham, through your offspring all peoples on earth will be blessed." Through Father Abraham came multiple generations of sons and daughters leading us to the blessing God spoke about, the Savior of John 3:16, "For God so loved the world that He gave His only begotten Son that whosoever believeth in Him shall not perish but shall have everlasting life."*

What is most magnificent and beyond full comprehension is our unity as sons and daughters of the Most High God as we, the body of believers, are the true family of Christ! And so it came to pass,

> In the sixth month, God sent the angel Gabriel to Nazareth, a town in Galilee, to a virgin pledged to be married to a man named Joseph, a descendant of David. The virgin's name was Mary. The angel went to her and said, "Greetings, you who are highly favored! The Lord is with you. ... Do not

be afraid, Mary, you have found favor with God. You will be with child and give birth to a son, and you are to give him the name Jesus (meaning Savior). He will be great and will be called the Son of the Most High. The Lord will give Him the throne of His father, David, and He will reign over the house of Jacob forever; His kingdom will never end." (Luke 1:26–33, LAB)

Jesus, the Savior that forever reigns was born in Bethlehem as was prophesied in Micah 5:2. Like any of us born today, the Christ Child's birth had to be recorded in a census. The life of baby Jesus had to be accounted for along with Joseph and Mary who were both descendants of the royal line of David. The Messiah's birth unfolds through Scripture:

> In those days Caesar Augustus issued a decree that a census should be taken ... and everyone went to his own town to register. So, Joseph also went up from the town of Nazareth in Galilee to Judea, to Bethlehem, the town of David, because he belonged to the house and line of David. He went there to register with Mary, who was pledged to be married to him and was expecting a child. While they were there, the time came for the baby to be born, and she gave birth to her firstborn, a son. She wrapped him in cloths and placed him in a manger, because there was no room for him in the inn.
>
> And there were shepherds living in the fields nearby, keeping watch over their flocks at night. An angel of the Lord appeared to them and the

glory of the Lord shone around them, and they were terrified. But the angel said to them, "Do not be afraid, I bring you great news of great joy that will be for all the people. Today in the town of David, a Savior has been born to you; he is Christ the Lord." (Luke 2:1–11 LAB)

Praise God! God sent us a Savior, His only begotten Son, who was born to die for us and to overcome sin and death so that we could be redeemed simply for opening our hearts and receiving this free gift of eternal life with our heavenly Father.

When Jesus was resurrected on the third day after He had been crucified, dead, and buried, He went to see the disciples. What message did Jesus have for them? He said, *"Peace be with you."* Jesus is the Prince of Peace. When He said, "Peace be with you," He was essentially saying *I Am* with you. Then Jesus ascended and went to sit at the right hand of God the Father until God frees Him to return for us, His bride. When we pray for the peace of Jerusalem, we are praying for the triumphant return of Christ, the Prince of Peace!

Jerry and I are blessed to have an olive tree planted in Israel. We gave $84.00 per month for one year to our local television station, Cornerstone Christian TV. We were able to do so with not much financial difficulty until the majority of positions had been eliminated from the company where Jerry used to work. Then it was challenging to write that check and send it; however, we kept our commitment with a heart of prayer for Israel and for the peace of Jerusalem, and God brought us through and blessed us. My heart is for the land of Israel to be undivided and ready for the return of *Jesus* because I am standing on the Word for the perfect will of God. In perfect timing, God gave Jerry another job and sold our home. In fact, God opened the door for our house to sale during a difficult economy and we did not use or have to pay for a realtor. Jerry and I then moved into a newly constructed house that had just been completed as we were ready to buy a new home. All that needed done was the seeding of the lawn. Let us be obedient to what God says ... even right here and now together in unity. Like sowing seed for grass to grow in my yard, let us sow and reap for the house of David and the house of the Lord, who has come and is coming again!

Join Israel in bringing God's light to the nations. Be God's flame in motion during these amazing times in God's plans for the world and believe that God will help you prosper. "Pray for the peace of Jerusalem: May they prosper who love you" (Psalm 122:6 NRSV).

Heavenly Father, hear our prayers in Jesus' name and to your glory! Thank You, Lord, for Your will to be done. Amen.

CHAPTER 10

Thy Kingdom Come,
Thy Will Be Done

You will receive power when my Holy Spirit comes on
you; and you will be my witnesses in Jerusalem, and in
all Judea and Samaria, and to the ends of the earth
—Acts 1: 8 LAB

In Esther 4:14 LAB, Mordecai states these words: "For if you remain silent at this time, relief and deliverance for the Jews will arise from another place, but you and your father's family will perish. And who knows but that you have come to royal position for such a time as this?" This verse reminds me that God is moving behind the scenes even when we cannot see what He is doing. God continues to prepare and call upon us to serve Him in faith for such a time as this. God continues to order our footsteps, direct our paths, make crooked paths straight, bring down mountains and purify, perfect, and teach us to serve Him. As we consider the story of Esther alongside our own stories, we can be at peace and trust God as we press on in the specific purpose, calling, and ministry God has for us. With the help of

His Holy Spirit, we are the hope of glory with Christ in us. We are His witnesses in Jerusalem and to the ends of the earth. Praise God because He is faithful to complete the good work He has begun in all of us and He is faithful to remain with us. Hold onto your faith for such a time as this.

God redeemed the Israelites from their slavery to Egypt. He redeemed us from our sins and from our worldly ways of living. More specifically, God saved me from the slavery of my sins. He cares about all of us and wants us for Himself, and He will orchestrate everything in our lives for the good of all according to His kingdom, which was, is, and is to come. He will use every detail of our lives to glorify Himself and bring us unto Himself. God wants a relationship with us, and He lights every step of our way to bring that relationship into being. In John 14:6, Jesus says, "I am the way, the truth, and the life. No one comes to the Father except through me." God had a plan for us so that He would be our God and we would be His people. He loves us with an everlasting love and has prepared a place for us to live with Him through all of eternity. God performs miracles daily on our behalf. Because God is such a living part of my life as He has been with others down through the ages, I give Him all the praise and glory for the things He has done.

What is to come? Let us take a look at John. He is referred to as the eagle (see Revelation 4:7) because of its ability to look directly at the sun. John looked directly at the Son and saw Christ as He really was. He wrote the book of Revelation as well as the book of John. His two underlying themes of being in Jesus include the following: (1) light and (2) life (John 1:4).

Most every morning that my mom in the Lord and I were at the ocean the week before the Fall semester 2011 began, God was showing Himself and His light off so beautifully as He would choose a spot out on the water and gradually move His light closer to us. The light of Christ seemed to shine right into our path from out on the ocean to our very balcony as we would read the Bible, pray, take Communion, and praise God each morning. It is interesting that the view would widen the farther out into the ocean I would look, but as I think about how God places His light on the distant water, it seemed that His light increased as it reached to our balcony in a similar way. It seemed that His light became more intense as it reached out to touch us and brighten our morning with its powerful rays.

When John the Baptist saw Jesus (see John 1:6–29, LAB), he said, "Look, the Lamb of God who takes away the sin of the world." However tempting it is to look to others, we must look to Jesus for our faith walk. Jesus guides us out of darkness and into His light (see John 1:9). John the Baptist calls himself the friend of the bridegroom (*shoshben*, meaning best man as seen in John 3:28–9). The best man would go in a room with the bride. When he heard the knock on the door from the groom, the best man would let the groom in and usher him to the bride. John the Baptist heard God knock and ushered Jesus to the bride. We are the twentieth-century *shoshben* preparing the Bride for the coming of the bridegroom, the church to Jesus. The light of the world in Christ could now be seen by those with eyes to see.

I remember that when I was growing up, I wanted glasses because I thought I could be cool like my older brother. I stared at the lightbulb in our TV room's lamp—not a smart thing to do. Our eyes are not made to look directly into light, and yet we are to be the carriers of God's light, pointing to the one true light: "Look, the Lamb of God!" John 14:6 says, "Jesus said, 'I am the way, the truth and the life. No one comes to the Father except through me.'" Yes, we mistakenly look at others like the people did with John the Baptist because we are so eager for the Savior to return to this earth once again, but there is only one true light: "Come, Lord Jesus" (Revelation 22:20 LAB).

As I come to the completion of this book, I pray that God uses it to turn our eyes all the more toward Jesus! The happenings that go on all around us from news to relationships to jobs (or whatever it is that takes our focus) often comes crashing in to rob us of our peace in Jesus. Along my journey in writing, many outside distractions have literally tried to thwart my progress. The obstacles in my way and the internal sense of resistance I have felt in trying to get the message onto paper show me that there is something worthwhile communicated in *Flame in Motion*. During a recent Florida vacation, I was talking with God about everything that troubled me in contrast to the peaceful surroundings of my friend's lanai. I sensed Him gently take my chin in His hand and have me look into His eyes. He was saying to let go of all of the stuff that is going on around me because at the essence of what matters most is Him and me. What matters most is the amazingly intimate relationship that our Savior wants to have with each one of us. Jesus is our light. He longs to gently hold all of our faces in His hand so that we intimately gaze into our Savior's eyes. When Jesus comes, all eyes will be on Him, for He is the light of the world!

> There will be no more night. They will not need the light of a lamp or the light of the sun for the Lord God will give them light. And they will reign forever and ever! ... Behold I am coming soon! My reward is with me, and I will give to everyone according to what he has done. I am the Alpha and Omega, the First and the Last, the Beginning and the End. Blessed are those who wash their robes, that they may have the right to

the tree of life and go through the gates into the city. Outside are the dogs, those who practice magic arts, the sexually immoral, the murderers, the idolaters and everyone who loves and practices falsehood. I am the Root and the offspring of David, and the bright Morning Star. The Spirit and the bride say, "Come!" And let him who hears say, "Come!" Whoever is thirsty, let him come; and whoever wishes, let him take the free gift of the water of life ... The grace of the Lord Jesus be with God's people. Amen. (Revelation 22:5, 12–17, 21 LAB)

So we must consider the following: "Arise, shine, for your light has come, and the glory of the Lord rises upon you!" (Isaiah 60:1 LAB). In Isaiah 62:1,11, I reiterate (as we continue to pray for the peace of Jerusalem) the prophet Isaiah's persistent prayer, "For Zion's sake, I will not keep silent, for Jerusalem's sake I will not remain quiet, till her righteousness shines out like the dawn, her salvation like a blazing torch ... The Lord has made proclamation to the ends of the earth: 'Say to the Daughter of Zion, See your Savior comes.'" We do not know the exact date when the Prince of Peace returns, but this I know: There are present day fathers of the faith passing down their mantle to a new generation with true hearts for our covenant connection to Israel. In July of this year, 2013, my NY Pastor, Bishop Tommy Reid who interviewed Robert Stearns of Eagles' Wings in 2010 regarding Jerusalem (as shared in the previous chapter) has been honored for 50 years of service as an apostolic leader and visionary. It is no mere coincidence that Robert Stearns, with such a heart for God and for God's Holy City, has received impartation and has stepped into the Bishop's Tabernacle role of church leadership.

I am far from a perfect carrier of God's light, but I have been willing not to hide His light in the writing of this book and in my life. Remember the little Sunday school song? "This little light of mine, I'm gonna to let it shine, let it shine, let it shine, let it shine." During my church worship this summer, 2013, I saw in my mind's eye a lit torch. As I looked upon its powerful flame, the fire became a dove representing the Holy Spirit. By God's Holy Spirit, we will light the way of the second coming of Christ to God's glory.

Heavenly Father, help me and help each of us to let Your light shine. Help us to point to You in all circumstances and to look up because as we look to You we shine Your light, Your Word, and Your truth, bringing the good news of salvation to your people. Lord, I pray for the peace of Jerusalem. Come, Lord Jesus! In Your holy name I pray, Jesus, return to us our Lord and Savior, light of the world! Amen.

FLAME IN MOTION

To overcome, to truly rise above, to blaze beyond
the atmosphere and reach for treasures of
Unknown galaxies while shining like stars in the
universe, is to simply be a carrier of God's glory.

Like sunlight shining through a crystal, a prism of
colors born of a bright white light flickers off
Walls, ceilings and floors making tangible the
intangible with brilliance only God can create.

For the crystal is only a carrier of His greater
ways. His steady light shines through you.
Wildfire or controlled flame depends upon the container of
light's dependence; yours on the One and only true God.

God knows the end from the beginning. He is the
Alpha, the Omega and the bright morning
Star, Himself. His inspiration bursts forth beyond
the limitations of our finite beings into infinity.

An eternity is that which only He can claim to own
and freely give to those who believe. He is the
Holy One, the Almighty, the triumphant Savior,
maker of heaven and earth, and Lord of our lives.

God pours through us lasting impressions of His
image to impart even in the absence of His
intense brilliance, His glow in you remains as I turn to
see you standing there, having been with Him—

Now with me I see your smile radiate as His
light bursts through your eyes. The vivid
Illumination is not easy to forget and who would want to?
I long to linger in His presence and I do as I see God—

in your countenance. Once again He is there, then
yet again from glory to glory. Nothing on
Earth compares. Abide with Him where the Creator of
your being makes your heart pure and Spirit-filled.

Shine, really shine the way that He alone can light
you up and send you forth anointed by His
touch, His face, His mercy, His grace, like that day I
turned to look at you and saw Him living through you.

Go forth and shine the way you did, the way you
were and the way you are in Him and with Him
in you. Rise above and shine, my love, Shine like stars
in the universe. You are His flame in motion.

—Written by Denise Stewart on 9/3/07

BIBLIOGRAPHY

Hamon, W.S. "Dr. Bill." *Apostles, Prophets and the Coming Moves of God*. Shippensburg: Destiny Image Publishers, Inc., 1997, p 8, 9, 12, 13, 19, 20, and 247.

Haverland, Kelita. Reference made to "Bella." Whitewater Productions, 2010, Heart of a Woman CD.

Ivey, A., D'Andrea, M., Ivey, M., & Simek-Morgan, L.. *Theories of Counseling and Psycohotherapy*; A Multicultural Perspective, 5th edition. Boston: Allyn and Bacon, A Pearson Education Company, 2002, p xvii.

Robison, James & Richards, Jay. *Indivisible*; Restoring Faith, Family and Freedom Before It's Too Late. New York: FaithWords, A division of Hachette Book Group, Inc., 2012, p 312.

Stewart, Denise. Finding the Way; A Journey Through Abuse, Therapeutic Brilliance and Blunders, to Healing. Mobile: Gazelle Press, 2005, p ix, x and xi.

Tomlin, Chris. Reference made to "Our God." Sparrow Records, 2010, Pasion: Awakening CD.

Trinity Christian Television, Living Epistles, Host Bishop Tommy Reid, Overflow Productions, a ministry of the Tabernacle, Orchard Park, NY, Show 552, 2010.

Veysey, Laurence. *The Emergence of the American University.* Chicago: The University of Chicago, 1965, p 21-56.

Weirsbe, Warren. *Be Restored*; Trusting God to See Us Through. Colorado Springs: David C. Cook, 2002, p 66, 81 and 93.

Welton, Jonathan. *The School of the Seers.* Shippensburg: Destiny Image Publishers, Inc., 2009, p 183 and 185.

"This Little Light of Mine," Addison Road, last accessed September 26, 2013, http://www.godtube.com/watch/?v=92MC91NU.

Genealogy Information, Mareen Duvall Descendants, last accessed September 26, 2013, http://www.geni.com/projects/ Descendants-of-Mareen-Duvall-of-Middle-Plantation.

Genealogy Information, Duvall and Denune Descendants, last accessed September 26, 2013, http://www.denune.org/ and http://www.denune.org/pdf/obama.pdf/.

ABOUT THE AUTHOR

Denise Stewart received her ministry license from Greater Works Outreach Bible School upon her graduation in May 2012. Prior to focusing her education to further embrace Jesus Christ through ministry, Denise earned a master's degree from the State University of New York at Buffalo in student personnel administration with a specialization in counseling and student development. Her internships have included campus ministry and educational development counseling in higher education. Denise also has a bachelor's degree in psychology from the University of Pittsburgh. She was a caseworker in foster care agencies for children and youth, and she worked with Big Brothers/Big Sisters of Pennsylvania as well. Her first book, *Finding the Way: A Journey through Abuse, Therapeutic Brilliance, and Blunders to Healing*, was published in November 2005 by Gazelle Press, a division of Genesis Communications in Mobile, AL. Denise continues to share her writing with a sincere heart for others, a deep desire to fulfill the plans and purposes God has for her life, and a devotion to shine light on our heavenly Father and His kingdom that is and is to come, all to His glory.

Denise has also served as a treasurer for the Westmoreland Association of Volunteer Administrators, and she was active in the Westmoreland County Teen Pregnancy Prevention Coalition. Earlier in her career, Denise worked in retail management, volunteered as a crisis counselor, and served as a contact person for an adult survivor of childhood sexual abuse self-help group. She has spent her life worshipping and serving God through numerous church-related ministries and activities, often with a focus on women's ministry. She has also been trained and has served as a Stephen minister. Denise and her husband, Jerry, enjoy the ocean and especially love spending time with their daughters, grandchildren, and extended family of God.

**To contact Denise Stewart
or to place an order for *Flame in Motion*,**
visit her website: www.findingtheway.net.